DORSET WALKS FOR MOTORISTS

G000122471

Warne Gerrard Guides for Walkers

Walks for Motorists Series

CHESHIRE WALKS
CHILTERNS WALKS
           Northern
           Southern
COTSWOLD WALKS
           Northern
           Southern
COUNTY OF AVON WALKS
COUNTY OF DURHAM WALKS
DARTMOOR WALKS
DERBYSHIRE WALKS
           Northern
           Southern
DORSET WALKS
ESSEX WALKS
EXMOOR WALKS
FAMILY WALKS IN MIDLAND COUNTIES
FURTHER CHESHIRE WALKS
FURTHER DALES WALKS
GREEN LONDON WALKS (both circular and cross country)
HAMPSHIRE AND THE NEW FOREST WALKS
HERTFORDSHIRE WALKS
ISLE OF WIGHT WALKS
JERSEY WALKS
KENT WALKS
LAKE DISTRICT WALKS
           Central
           Northern
           Western
LOTHIAN AND SOUTH EAST BORDERS WALKS
MIDLAND WALKS
NORTHUMBERLAND WALKS
NORTH YORK MOORS WALKS
           North and East
           West and South
PEAK DISTRICT WALKS
PENDLESIDE AND BRONTE COUNTRY WALKS
SEVERN VALLEY WALKS
SNOWDONIA WALKS Northern
SOUTH DEVON WALKS
SOUTH DOWNS WALKS
SURREY WALKS
WYE VALLEY WALKS
YORKSHIRE DALES WALKS

Long Distance and Cross Country Walks

RAMBLES IN THE DALES
WALKING THE PENNINE WAY

DORSET

WALKS FOR MOTORISTS

Roberta MacLaren

30 circular walks
with sketch maps by F. Rodney Fraser

FREDERICK WARNE

Published by
Frederick Warne (Publishers) Ltd
40 Bedford Square,
London WC1B 3HE

The photographs on the front and back cover are of Corfe Castle. The front cover picture was taken by Derek Forss; the back cover picture appears by kind permission of Leonard Gayton.

Publishers' Note

While every care has been taken in the compilation of this book, the publishers cannot accept responsibility for any inaccuracies. Things may have changed since the book was published: paths are sometimes diverted, a concrete bridge may replace a wooden one, stiles disappear. Please let the publishers know if you discover anything like this on your way.

The length of each walk in this book is given in miles and kilometres, but within the text Imperial measurements are quoted. It is useful to bear the following approximations in mind: 5 miles = 8 kilometres, $\frac{1}{2}$ mile = 805 metres, 1 metre = 39.4 inches.

ISBN 0 7232 2143 X

Phototypeset by Tradespools Ltd, Frome, Somerset
Printed by Galava Printing Co. Ltd, Nelson, Lancashire

Contents

			Page
		Introduction	7
Walk	1	Hengistbury Head	11
	2	Pentridge	14
	3	Cranborne Chase	17
	4	Shell Bay	20
	5	Studland	23
	6	The Purbeck Hills	26
	7	Badbury Rings	29
	8	Worth Matravers	31
	9	Corfe Castle	34
	10	Houns-tout and Chapman's Pool	37
	11	Ashmore	40
	12	Tarrant Crawford	42
	13	Ibberton Hill and Turnworth	45
	14	Milton Abbas	48
	15	Lulworth Cove and Durdle Door	51
	16	Hilton	54
	17	Ringstead Bay and Durdle Door	57
	18	The Dorsetshire Gap	61
	19	Puddletown Forest	64
	20	Osmington Mills	67
	21	The Heart of the Hardy Country	70
	22	White Horse Hill	73
	23	Portland	75
	24	Maiden Castle	78
	25	Sherborne Deer Park	81
	26	Cerne Abbas and Up Cerne	83
	27	Fleet	87
	28	The Hardy Monument	90
	29	Golden Cap	93
	30	Stonebarrow Hill	95

DORSET

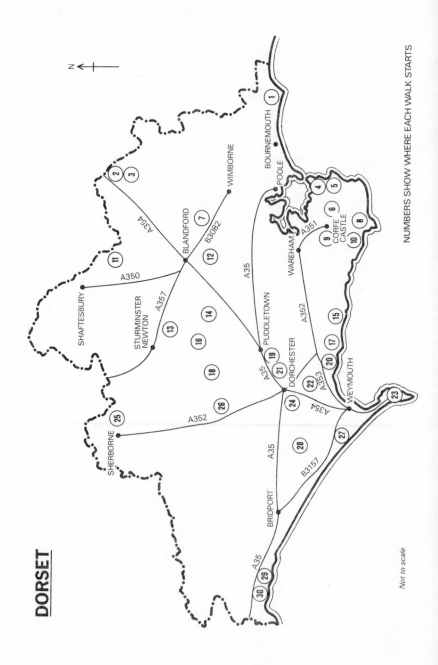

N

NUMBERS SHOW WHERE EACH WALK STARTS

Not to scale

Introduction

Compared with many, Dorset is not a large county yet it must be one of the most charming and interesting in England. Situated about midway along the south coast, it is bordered by Hampshire to the east, Devon to the west and Somerset and Wiltshire to the north. Each of these counties has its own form of beauty but Dorset shares them all.

In the eastern corner of the county is Cranborne Chase (see Walks 2 and 3), an area of rolling chalk downland strongly reminiscent of Wiltshire's Salisbury Plain. Here the high, open country provides panoramic views. There are surprisingly few houses and the villages are small and isolated. One of them, Ashmore (see Walk 11), is the highest village in Dorset.

From Cranborne Chase the chalk hills stretch west towards Beaminster and the Devon and Somerset borders. They include the two highest hills in Dorset, Pilsdon Pen near Broadwindsor and Bulbarrow (see Walk 16), both of which are over 900 ft high. Amongst these chalk hills are some of the most beautiful and unfrequented parts of the county, such as the area around the Dorsetshire Gap (see Walk 18) where the walker has the opportunity to enjoy the peaceful heart of rural Dorset with its wide variety of flora and fauna.

From Beaminster another line of chalk hills runs south-west to skirt Dorchester and end in the tall, white cliffs that add so much to the beauty of the Dorset coast. White Nothe (see Walk 17) is the most western place where these hills reach the sea. Further east they swing inland again to form the northern boundary of Purbeck (see Walks 6 and 9) before ending in the beautiful headland called Ballard Point. Here the white cliffs and Old Harry rock strongly resemble the Needles and the cliffs of Freshwater Bay on the Isle of Wight.

As in other counties, the chalk hills of Dorset have their share of carvings. Cerne Abbas Giant (see Walk 26) is one of the most famous hill-figures in England. It is the portrait of a nude man brandishing a club and is 180 ft in height. Its age is unknown but it is certainly very old. Some say it dates from Roman times and portrays the god Hercules, others that it was first cut during the Dissolution of the Monasteries and is a very uncomplimentary caricature of the last abbot. Probably the most likely theory is that it was cut into the turf long before the Romans came to Britain and represents an ancient British god.

Unlike the Cerne Abbas Giant, the age of the figure cut into the turf of White Horse Hill near Weymouth (see Walk 22) is known exactly. This is a comparatively young hill-carving. It was cut in 1808 under the direction of a local bookseller. The figure represents King George

III on his horse and commemorates that monarch's connection with the town of Weymouth.

Beyond the chalk uplands in the south-east corner of the county is an area where heathland similar to that found in Hampshire's New Forest abounds. This is the part of Dorset which the novelist Thomas Hardy (see Walk 21) called Egdon Heath. It encircles the great expanse of water known as Poole Harbour (see Walk 4) and is fringed on its coastal border by the golden sands of Bournemouth beach and Shell Bay. Not all of it is open heathland. Some parts of it are farm land, others, such as Puddletown Forest (see Walk 19), are woodland and the majority of the extreme south-eastern corner is swallowed up in the sprawling townships of Poole and Bournemouth.

On the south-western side of the county there are no large towns. Here the soil is clay and the scenery strongly resembles that found in Devon. High banks and hedges line the lanes, the cottages are built of stone and herds of dairy cattle graze in the fields. The coastline is rugged and very beautiful with tall multi-coloured cliffs, one of which, Golden Cap (see Walks 29 and 30), is the highest on the south coast of England.

Further east the cliffs give way to the Chesil Beach (see Walk 27). This is a huge bank of shingle which stretches from Bridport to Portland, a distance of about 18 miles. To begin with it is connected to the mainland, but east of Abbotsbury it becomes an actual bank and encloses a narrow salt-water lake called the Fleet.

East of Weymouth the cliffs begin again. Here are to be found a variety of picturesque beaches and coves hidden amongst the folds of the coastline. Osmington Mills (see Walk 20) is a particularly beautiful example. A small stream runs through a deep-sided valley to the sea, and the view of Weymouth Bay is almost as it was when John Constable painted it. Further east, in the Isle of Purbeck, another stream runs down to the sea at Chapman's Pool (see Walk 10). This is a small and secluded bay which is shielded to the west by the ridge of land that ends in Houns-tout Cliff.

On the stretch of coastline between Osmington Mills and Chapman's Pool lie Lulworth Cove and Durdle Door (see Walk 15). These are two very well known Dorset beauty spots. Durdle Door is a natural arch of stone which stands in the sea and is joined to the mainland by a narrow isthmus. Lulworth Cove is an almost perfectly circular bay enclosed by high cliffs with a narrow opening to the sea. It has been a popular place with visitors for well over a hundred years. Keats spent his last day in England here and it was here that he wrote his last sonnet. Rupert Brooke also loved it. It was whilst boating here that he dropped his copy of Keats poems overboard and was forced to take a ducking in order to retrieve it.

Other than the islands in Poole Harbour there are no real islands along the Dorset coast. Yet Dorset has two areas which are called islands and are not. One is the Isle of Purbeck which is only an island in that it is separated from the rest of the county by a ridge of hills flanked by open heathland. The other is the Isle of Portland which is really a peninsula joined to the mainland by the Chesil Beach.

Both of these 'islands' are renowned for their quarrying. In Purbeck (see Walk 8) a creamy grey stone is to be found and most of the local houses are built of it. A blackish-green marble was also quarried here at one time. It was used in many medieval churches and cathedrals including the one at Salisbury. Portland stone is even more famous. It has been used in many well known buildings including Whitehall Palace, St Paul's Cathedral and London University.

Portland (see Walk 23) is a fascinating place. Crouching like a massive stone monster in the sea to the west of Weymouth, it is unlike anything else in Dorset and must be one of the strangest pieces of country in England. Its high plateau is practically treeless and its rocky cliffs have a unique and wild grandeur.

Yet it is not only the beauty of its scenery and the magnificence of its coastline that make Dorset such an interesting county. It also has a lot to offer to those who enjoy history. Together with its neighbour Wiltshire, Dorset has a greater number and variety of early monuments and earthworks than any other county in southern England. Many of these earthworks are the remains of formidable hill-forts which were built long before the Romans came to Britain. They include Badbury Rings (see Walk 7), Hambledon Hill (see Walk 13), Spettisbury Rings (see Walk 12) and Maiden Castle (see Walk 24). Maiden Castle has been described as the largest and most perfect earthwork in the world. It is certainly the biggest in England. The majority of its ramparts were built by a tribe known as the Durotriges who were also responsible for the fortification of Hengistbury Head (see Walk 1).

Besides early earthworks Dorset also has its share of Saxon and Norman buildings, the most famous of which must surely be Corfe Castle (see Walk 9). It was here, in the year 978, that the young King Edward, who later became known as Edward the Martyr, met his death at the hands of his stepmother Queen Elfrida.

Dorset has no cathedral city but before the Dissolution of the Monasteries it was well endowed with religious foundations, some of which, such as the abbey at Cerne Abbas (see Walk 26), were of great importance. The abbey at Tarrant Crawford (see Walk 12) was founded by Bishop Poore who also built Salisbury Cathedral. Three other abbeys, those at Sherborne, Milton Abbas and Wimborne Minster, have given the county its three great churches.

The abbey church at Milton Abbas (see Walk 14) stands beside one of the county's old stately homes. Milton, which is now a public school, is the only large house in Dorset to keep its original design. It was built in 1771 by a despot who destroyed a whole market town in order to lay out his park and then erected the uniquely beautiful village of Milton Abbas to take its place.

During the demolition of the market town of Milton Abbas one of England's oldest grammar schools was destroyed. It once stood beside the abbey church and numbered amongst its pupils Admiral

Sir Thomas Masterman Hardy. Admiral Hardy came from Portesham (see Walk 28) and was the captain of Nelson's flagship at the battle of Trafalgar.

Another of the county's large houses, Sherborne Castle (see Walk 25), was built by Sir Walter Raleigh. After his disgrace it came into the possession of the Digby family. Its beautiful park and artificial lake were laid out by 'Capability' Brown who also laid out the gardens and park at Milton.

With the exception of the quarrying in Purbeck and Portland and the industry in Poole, Dorset is predominantly an agricultural county. This fact, which has helped to preserve its beauty and so much evidence of its past, also imposes certain responsibilities on the walker. Always follow the Country Code.

The Country Code

Guard against fire risks
Fasten all gates
Keep dogs under proper control
Keep to the paths across farm land
Avoid damaging fences, hedges and walls
Leave no litter
Safeguard water supplies
Protect wild life, wild plants and trees
Go carefully on country roads
Respect the life of the countryside.

All the cliff paths used in the walks were perfectly safe at the time of writing, but it is never wise to walk at the very edge of a cliff or to climb it. Because of their structure, Dorset cliffs are notoriously crumbly and accidents happen every year because foolish people disregard the warning notices.

Although every attempt has been made to avoid boggy places, patches of mud or rough ground are inescapable. Boots and thick socks are advisable both for comfort and in order to avoid the twisted ankles which can so easily mar a pleasant outing.

The sheet number of the appropriate 1:50,000 Ordnance Survey map is given at the heading of each walk.

Walk 1   Hengistbury Head

3 miles (4·5 km)

OS sheet 195
Start: Hengistbury Head car park

Hengistbury Head is a relatively new Dorset beauty spot having come
into the county from Hampshire during the recent boundary changes.
It is a lofty headland covered with open heath, and forms the southern
border of Christchurch Harbour. This is a particularly beautiful
stretch of water which provides a sheltered haven for a variety of small
sailing dinghies and other pleasure craft. Swans abound here and
heron are sometimes to be seen amongst the reeds which line the
water's edge.

Christchurch Harbour is the estuary of two large rivers: the Avon,
which flows through Hampshire, and a Dorset river, the Stour. Their
waters meet at Christchurch and flow on from there through Christchurch Harbour to the sea. Good views of this piece of water are to be
obtained from the top of Warren Hill whilst, in the opposite direction,
Poole Bay curves west towards Poole Harbour.

Hengistbury Head has not always been the deserted stretch of grass
and heathland that it is today. In fact there were settlements here up
until the end of the fifth century when the Saxons founded the town of
Christchurch further up the river.

The earliest inhabitants were a tribe of reindeer hunters who came
from the Continent about 11,000 years ago and camped amongst the
sand-dunes which then covered Warren Hill. Their chief concern was
that their settlement was close to a ford used by the reindeer, but later
settlers chose to live here for a very different reason.

Being bordered on three sides by water, Hengistbury Head is easy
to defend. During the Iron Age the pair of ramparts known as Double
Dykes was built across the western end, thus turning the whole
headland into a promontory fort. The ramparts were built by a tribe
called the Durotriges who also built the formidable ramparts at
Maiden Castle near Dorchester.

Behind the Double Dykes a sizable town flourished. It grew into a
small but active port which served as an important link with the Continent but was eventually abandoned during the fourth century when
the number of Saxon raids on the south coast increased.

From central Bournemouth follow the signs to the Lansdowne and
Boscombe. Go straight through Boscombe shopping centre to

11

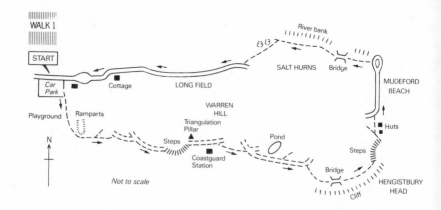

Pokesdown and, having passed Pokesdown station on the left, turn right at the traffic lights into Seabourne Road. Carry on until the shops are left behind and the road curves to the right. Here you will find the first of a series of road signs which indicate the way to Hengistbury Head. Just before the road ends there is a large car park on the right.

Leave the car park by the gap in the bank at the back left-hand corner and head diagonally right across the children's playground. This will bring you to a wire fence which encloses the end of the ramparts. At the far end of this fence turn left on to a gravel path which leads between the ramparts and the beach.

Follow this path straight ahead and where it divides keep to the right-hand fork. This crosses a stretch of grass and then joins another gravel track that leads up a slope. At this point there are good views to the left. The Stour and Avon estuary can be seen with Christchurch Priory in the distance.

At the top of the slope the path merges with another and swings to the right. Continue along it and then climb up the steps to the triangulation pillar. From here follow the path straight ahead passing the coastguard station on your right.

Just beyond the coastguard station the path divides. Keep to the right-hand fork which is grass-covered and leads straight ahead. It rejoins the gravel track at a point where this divides once more. Take the right-hand fork which goes down a slope passing a pond in the valley on the left. This narrow, steep-sided valley is part of the old ironstone quarry which was dug during the middle of the last century.

Ignore the path to the left on the far side of the valley and continue to follow the gravel one straight ahead. Leave it where it swings to the left and take the narrow path that skirts the edge of the cliff on the right. This path will take you over a plank bridge spanning a gully and then on up to the top of the cliffs at the end of the headland. From this point turn left to descend the steps to the beach.

12

At the bottom of the steps bear left to pass behind the beach huts. Then, where the path forks, keep to the right. This will bring you to a narrow, metalled lane. Follow this straight ahead to its end and then turn left to skirt the edge of the water on your right. This is Christchurch Harbour.

Cross the wooden bridge and carry on along the rather indistinct path which follows the water's edge. Just before the river bank swings left and becomes scrub-covered, turn left on to a narrow path that leads through the undergrowth. Follow this path to where it joins the lane and turn right. This will eventually bring you back to the road and the car park.

Walk 2   Pentridge

4 miles (6 km)

OS sheet 184
Start: Pentridge

Pentridge is a tiny hamlet hidden away in the rolling downland of Cranborne Chase. From the top of Pentridge Hill there are glorious views. To the south the walker can look down across the valley towards Cranborne, whilst to the north the panorama of hills and valleys which make up the area where Dorset and Wiltshire meet stretches away to the distant horizon.

Bokerley Ditch marks the border between Dorset and Hampshire. It was built during late Roman times to protect the area against invasion from the north-east, and at one time actually blocked the old Roman road which runs across the Chase.

For those who have a few moments to spare, Pentridge church, which marks the starting and finishing point of this walk, is well worth a visit. On the left-hand side of the aisle is to be found a memorial tablet to Robert Browning, who died in 1746 and was the poet's great-grandfather.

The only metalled road to Pentridge is a narrow lane which leaves the A354, Blandford to Salisbury road, between the Handley Hill roundabout and Woodyates. It is on the right coming from Blandford and is clearly marked. The lane winds its way down the hill to the village and turns sharp right at a point where another, minor lane joins it from the left. Keep following the lane round to the right, pass Trantridge Cottage on the left and then turn right opposite a large wooden barn on to a track which leads up to the church. Park on the edge of the grass to the right just beyond the church.

Go back down the track to the lane and turn right. Having passed the telephone kiosk, which is painted green, turn left to cross a stile and follow a narrow path, passing a tree on your right.

From here the path, which has become very faint, goes up the slope to a second stile at the top of the field. Cross this and walk on between the hedges to where another stile gives access to the open downland on Pentridge Hill.

Go straight up the hill to the group of fir trees on Penbury Knoll. There is no path but it is an easy climb. When you reach the trees, carry on through them and turn left on to a track which follows the fence near the far side. The track soon leaves the trees and runs along the ridge giving good views to left and right.

14

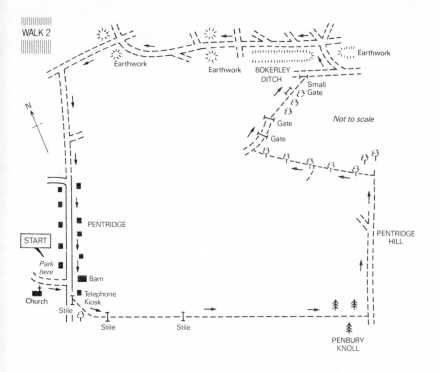

Eventually the track becomes indistinct and divides. Ignore the left-hand branch which follows the curve of the ridge and go straight on along the fence. This will lead you to a stand of trees in the corner of the field. Turn left beside them to follow a line of hawthorns across the hillside. A narrow path leads to the left beside the third tree, but disregard it and carry on to pass another two trees and reach a track. Turn right here and follow the track through the gate.

Within a very short distance this will bring you to a second gate. Do not go through it, but pass to the right of it and follow the fence to the left. This will eventually lead you down a narrow path between the fence and a line of bushes on the right. Pass a gate on the left and carry on to another, smaller gate in the bottom left-hand corner of the field. Go through this and turn right on to the track beyond.

After a few hundred yards the track merges with another from the left. Turn sharp left on to this and follow it down through a line of ramparts to where it divides four ways. Take the extreme left-hand fork which follows the side of the earthwork. This earthwork is Bokerley Ditch and you are now skirting the county boundary with Hampshire to your right.

Follow the track down the hill passing two other tracks on the right.

15

In the valley it is crossed by a third track, but ignore this and carry straight on up the slope to where the track cuts through a small earth-work and divides. Take the left-hand fork. This soon merges with another track from the left and winds along beside Bokerley Ditch before swinging right to climb a slight slope. At the top of the slope it is crossed by another track. Turn left on to this.

The track cuts through the earthwork, passing a National Nature Reserve sign on the left, then runs between fields for some distance before swinging left and dividing. At this point take the left fork. It steadily becomes more distinct and eventually merges with a lane. Follow the lane straight ahead to where it joins the major lane at Cross Cottage and then carry straight on to reach the track which leads up to the church on the right.

Walk 3   Cranborne Chase

3½ miles (5·5 km)

OS sheets 184 and 185
Start: Squirrel's Corner

Cranborne Chase is an area of open downland to the east of
Blandford. It is a beautiful place, very similar in character to
Salisbury Plain and equally well endowed with archaeological
remains. Besides the profusion of Bronze Age round barrows which
stud its fields there are a number of interesting earthworks. Two of
these are Ackling Dyke and the Dorset Cursus.

The Dorset Cursus was built in Neolithic times as a line of defence.
It consists of a pair of parallel banks set 270 ft apart and flanked by
ditches. Today much of it has vanished beneath the plough but a
section is still to be seen where it is crossed by the B3081 at Bottlebush
Down.

Ackling Dyke is a Roman road which once ran between Salisbury
and Badbury Rings. It is one of the best examples of an embanked
Roman road in the country and in places the bank is over 6 ft high.

Cranborne Chase gets its name from the fact that it was once a
royal hunting preserve. It was first set aside for this purpose by
William the Conqueror and the restrictions he imposed on the pursuit
of game in the area were not lifted until 1828.

During the eighteenth and nineteenth centuries these unpopular
restrictions were the cause of a great deal of lawlessness. Bands of
poachers armed with vicious jointed cudgels roamed the Chase and
often came to blows with the keepers. Many of these poachers were
not poor people who went poaching from necessity but wealthy young
bloods who resented the ban on hunting and considered poaching an
exciting and permissible alternative.

Take the A354 from Blandford heading towards Salisbury and turn
right at the Handley Hill roundabout on to the B3081 which is signposted to Cranborne. Follow the B3081 for a fifth of a mile. Having
passed two tracks on the right, you come to where a wood approaches
the road. Beside it a third track joins the road. This is Squirrel's
Corner. Turn right and park on the grass beside this track.

Follow the track which cuts through the trees and then becomes
grass-covered as it winds its way between the fields.

After a while the wheel ruts become more distinct and the track,
which is now bordered by hedges, leads downhill. Near the bottom of

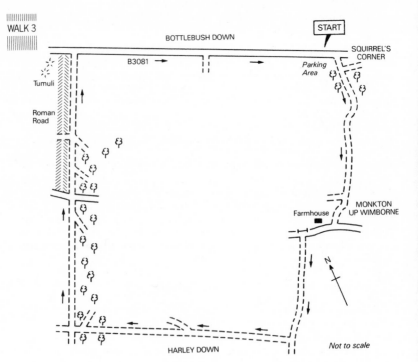

the slope it is joined by a second track which comes from some farm buildings to the right. Ignore this and carry straight on until you reach the road.

Turn right and follow the road as it curves past a white farmhouse on the right. Directly opposite the farm entrance a track leads away to the left. Turn left and follow it across a stretch of water, parts of which are piped, and up a hill. At the top of the hill turn right on to a track which leads towards a belt of trees.

After some distance this track forks, but the right-hand branch just goes through some bushes to a field, so keep to the left. Follow it up to the trees and pass through them, ignoring a track which leads away to the right. On the far side of the trees the track crosses a bridleway. Turn right on to this and follow it down the slope beside the wood.

Initially there are magnificent views across the fields to the left but nearer the bottom of the slope these are obstructed by a hedge. A track emerges from amongst the trees on the right and almost immediately the bridleway joins the road.

Cross the road and follow the grassy track which leads straight ahead. To the left of it is a fence and beyond this a bank covered with

18

bushes. This bank is part of the old Roman road known as Ackling Dyke.

For some distance the track is sandwiched between Ackling Dyke on the left and the wood on the right. It is joined at intervals by two minor tracks from the right but ignore both these and carry straight on. This will eventually bring you to a point where the track emerges from the trees, and the ridge of Ackling Dyke, now free of bushes, can be seen climbing the slope ahead. Another track cuts through the bank and heads towards the trees on the right, but ignore this and continue to follow the one which runs beside the Roman road.

At the top of the slope there are two tumuli in the field on the left. These are some of the Bronze Age round barrows which are to be found in such great numbers on the Chase. Beside them, on the ridge of Ackling Dyke, is one of the old milestones, although its surface is so weathered that the inscription has been obliterated.

Not far beyond this place the track comes to the road. Cross it and turn right to walk along the wide verge on the far side. This will eventually bring you to a point opposite the track where you left the car.

Walk 4   Shell Bay

4 miles (6 km)

OS sheet 195
Start: South Haven Point or Sandbanks beach

Studland Heath stretches north from Purbeck to embrace the peninsula of sand which separates Poole Harbour from the sea. This is a wild, uninhabited area, glorious in summer when the heather is in bloom but always beautiful.

To the west is Studland Bay with its wide sandy beaches leading down from a backdrop of dunes topped with marram grass. Behind them is a freshwater lake known as Little Sea. It is part of the Studland Heath National Nature Reserve and, during the winter months, is. visited by large numbers of waterfowl. The marshes around the lake make an excellent home for many species of dragonflies and all six kinds of British reptiles are to be found on the surrounding heath.

Part of the reserve has been laid out as a nature trail and this is well worth a visit. The path leads through woodland to the southern shore of the lake where hides have been provided so that visitors can watch the birds.

To the north of the peninsula the waters of Poole Harbour stretch away towards the Wareham river. There are good views of Brownsea Island, which is now a National Trust property, and of the smaller Furzey Island which lies to its south. Both these islands were once the haunt of smugglers who brought their goods across the peninsula and then, by way of the islands, to the inner parts of Dorset.

High on a hill in the centre of Studland Heath stands Agglestone. This is a curiously eroded sandstone rock, roughly 18 ft in height and 80 ft in girth, which is said to weigh over 400 tons. Its name means 'the Holy Stone' and, together with another smaller rock called Puckstone, it is believed to have featured in a religious cult which flourished in the area long before the Romans came to Britain.

Drive through Poole to Sandbanks and take the ferry to Shell Bay. Either leave the car in the car park at Sandbanks beach and walk down to the ferry or cross the ferry in the car and use the car park on the left at South Haven Point.

If you have parked at Sandbanks beach follow the road down to the ferry and cross it to reach South Haven Point car park.

Follow the road from South Haven Point car park until you come to

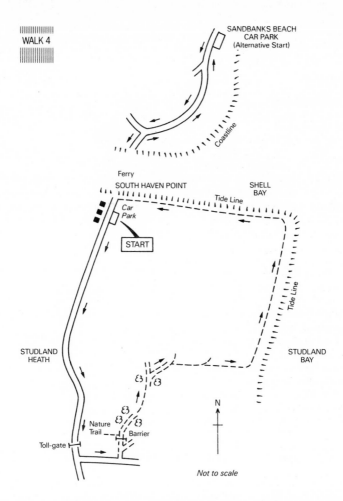

SANDBANKS BEACH
CAR PARK
(Alternative Start)

Coastline

Ferry
SOUTH HAVEN POINT

SHELL
BAY

Tide Line

Car
Park

START

Tide Line

STUDLAND
HEATH

STUDLAND
BAY

N

Nature
Trail

Barrier

Toll-gate

Not to scale

the toll-gate. This is a very long way but there is a wide verge and the views from the road make it well worth while. To start with the backwaters of Poole Harbour slowly unfold beyond the heathland to the right. It is from here that some of the best views of Brownsea Island are obtained.

Not far along the road the grounds of the Studland Heath National Nature Reserve border it on the left and there are glimpses of the stretch of water known as Little Sea. Then, as the backwaters of the harbour give way to heath on the right, the road goes round a left-hand bend and begins to descend a slope. Straight ahead at this point, out across the heath, the dark shape of Agglestone is clearly visible on its hill.

Having passed the toll-gate, turn left into the entrance to the beach car park. Just beyond the attendant's kiosk there is a track to the left. Follow this track to where it forks, then take the left-hand branch which leads straight ahead through the vehicle barrier.

Not far beyond the barrier the beginning of the nature trail is on the left. This trail is about half a mile in length and is certainly worth a detour as it is superbly laid out and provides an excellent opportunity to study the birds on Little Sea.

Having passed the beginning of the nature trail follow the track through the bushes to where it emerges on to a wide expanse of sand. Cross this and follow the track at the far side past some bushes on the right and some more on the left. Where the track forks take the right-hand branch which bears round to the right.

Ignore a path which goes through the fence to the left and carry on to where the fence ends. At this point the path swings left but leave it and go straight ahead across the dunes to the beach.

Turn left to follow the stretch of firmer sand just above the tide line. This will take you to the point where the water's edge swings left at the harbour mouth. Still continue to follow the tide line which is now leading you back towards the ferry.

At the ferry either turn left to return to South Haven Point car park or cross the ferry and follow the road back to Sandbanks beach car park.

Walk 5   Studland

3½ miles (5·5 km)

OS sheet 195
Start: Woodhouse

During the sixteenth century Studland was notorious for its pirates; today it is a popular seaside village. There are two beaches, the more southerly being smaller and stonier than its counterpart which is a wide expanse of soft golden sand. The sea is perfectly safe for bathing and the sheltered harbour provides an excellent anchorage for the multitude of small pleasure craft which visit the area during the summer.

The headland which separates Studland Bay from Swanage Bay possesses some of the most beautiful coastal scenery in the whole of Dorset. It is here that the high chalk hills that separate the Isle of Purbeck from Dorset's eastern heathland come to the sea. The last part of this line of hills is Ballard Down. It forms the backbone of the headland and from the top of it there are panoramic views across Poole Harbour and Swanage.

Ballard Down ends in the tall white cliffs of Ballard Point. To the north of this the cliffs stretch away to Handfast Point where the two stacks called Old Harry and Old Harry's Wife stand in the sea. This is a paradise for bird watchers. Gulls, cormorants and other sea-birds nest on the stacks and the cliff ledges whilst rooks and a variety of finches frequent the fields.

Take the A351 from Wareham to Purbeck and turn left opposite Corfe Castle on to the B3351 which is signposted to Studland. Having travelled down this road for about four miles you pass a turning on the left marked 'Woodhouse Hill'. Not far beyond this there is a lay-by on the right. It is marked by a blue board advertising the Bankes Arms Hotel.

Go back up the road for about fifty yards to where a path leads down the bank to the left. It is marked 'Footpath to Swanage'.

At the bottom of the bank the path passes through a fence where a special section made up of two horizontal wooden bars has been provided for the walker. The path then swings right and follows the side of the field towards a cottage. Beside the cottage there is another path which goes straight ahead. Ignore this and turn left to continue along the field boundary.

At the end of the cottage garden the path leaves the perimeter of the

23

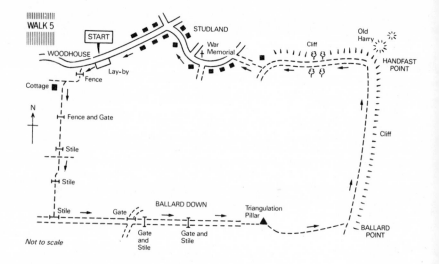

field and heads straight down the hill towards a gate and another two-bar section of fence like the one already encountered. Go over this and then straight ahead up the hill. This will bring you to a stile about two-thirds of the way up the slope. Cross it and, ignoring the path which runs along the hillside just beyond it, carry on up bearing slightly right to reach another stile on what initially looks like the hill crest. Beyond this stile the path leads straight on up the hill again to a third stile set on the ridge of Ballard Down.

Parts of the climb to this point are fairly steep but on arrival the walker is rewarded with the chance to pause and admire the magnificent views. Straight ahead are Swanage, Peveril Point and the hills around Durlston Head. In the opposite direction lies Poole Harbour with the town of Bournemouth in the far distance.

Having taken a suitable rest, cross the stile and turn left to follow the track along the ridge. After some distance it is crossed by a path. This emerges from a small gate to the left at a point where the main track is barred by a gate with a stile beside it. Disregard the path and go straight on passing through a second gate with a stile beside it to reach a place where the fence on the left ends and the track degenerates into a narrow path. This path leads to a triangulation pillar from where a grassy path bears away to the right heading for a fence post at the corner of a field. Turn on to this path. At the corner of the field it swings left and widens as it leads down a slope beside the fence.

At the bottom of the slope turn left to follow the path on along the cliff top. The two stacks known as Old Harry and Old Harry's Wife are straight ahead. Beside them the path swings left again to follow the cliff as it curves back towards Studland.

24

After passing Old Harry the path broadens into a track which goes through a group of trees and then on between fields. Eventually it curves to the left at a place where a gravel footpath leads straight ahead. Leave the track at this point and follow the path. It passes an interesting stone house to the right and then joins a track which slopes down to the road.

Turn left and follow the road. At the war memorial it curves to the right and is joined by a road from the church. Disregard this and follow the signpost to Studland village.

At the crossroads turn left and continue along the road which will take you back to the lay-by.

Walk 6   The Purbeck Hills

4½ miles (7 km)

OS sheet 195
Start: Brenscombe Hill

Brenscombe Hill and Nine Barrow Down form part of the barrier of chalk hills which run east from Arish Mell and end in the cliffs at Ballard Point. They are about 500 ft in height, and from the top there are wonderful views of Purbeck and the surrounding country.

Near the beginning of the walk there is a view to the left across Godlingston Heath to Poole Harbour and Brownsea Island. Poole Harbour, which is the second largest natural harbour in the world, contains several islands of which Brownsea is the largest. It is a densely wooded island with a shore line over three miles in length. During its chequered history it has been inhabited by the Romans, harried by Canute and owned by the monks of Cerne Abbey. Over 400 years ago a castle was built on it to defend Poole Harbour, but this was given by Elizabeth I to her favourite, Sir Christopher Hatton, who used its guns to extract toll money from all the ships entering the harbour. Brownsea also played a part in the birth of the Boy Scout movement for it was on this island in 1907 that Lord Baden-Powell held the first Boy Scout camp. Today the island is owned by the National Trust and is preserved as a bird sanctuary.

During the last part of the walk Corfe Castle is to be seen. This impressive Norman ruin stands on a mound in the centre of the only gap in the line of chalk hills.

Take the B3351 road from Corfe Castle travelling towards Studland. After about two miles a road to Rempstone Farm leads away to the left, and directly opposite it is a gravel track. Turn on to the track and park on the right beside it. This is the foot of Brenscombe Hill.

Pass through the gap beside the gate and carry on up the track. Where the track forks take the left-hand branch which soon leaves the trees, passes through a gate and continues up the hill. It passes through another group of trees to reach the ridge from where there are good views of Poole Harbour and Brownsea Island to the left.

On the ridge the track ends. Turn right at this point and cross a stile to reach another track on the far side. Turn left and follow the track up the slope to where it divides, then take the left-hand fork.

This track leads to a gate. Just before it turn right on to a narrow path. This swings round to pass a tumulus on the left before curving

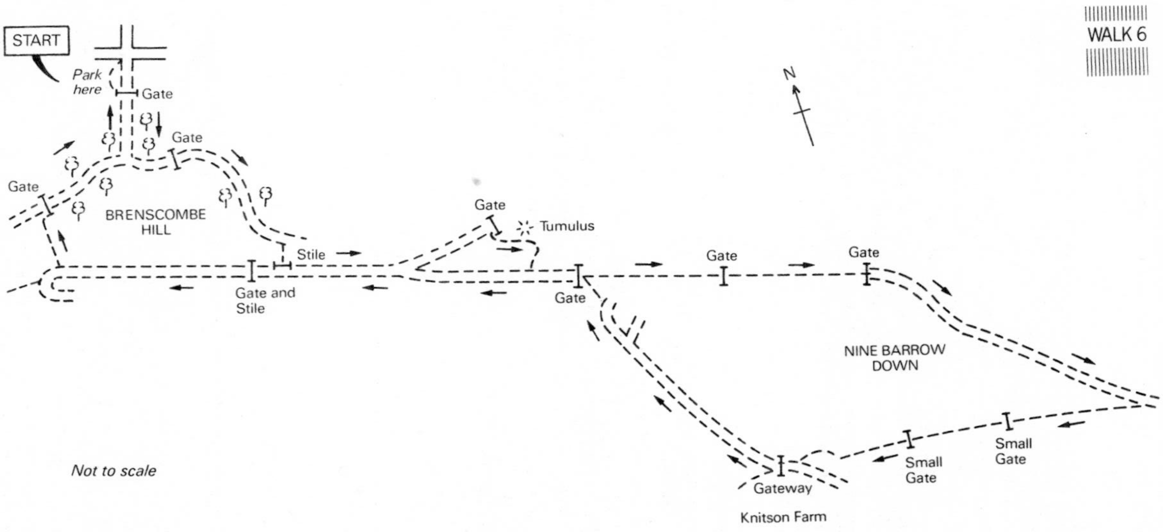

WALK 6

N

START

Park here

Gate

BRENSCOMBE HILL

Gate

Gate

Stile

Gate and Stile

Gate

Tumulus

Gate

Gate

Gate

NINE BARROW DOWN

Gateway

Knitson Farm

Small Gate

Small Gate

Not to scale

right and running down beside a fence to join another track. Turn left on to this track which eventually ends at a gate. Go through the gate and carry straight on to a second gate near the top of the rise. Beyond this go straight on again to another gate and then follow the track down the slope.

Near the bottom the track is joined by a path from the right. Turn sharp right on to this. It follows the fence on the left and passes through two small gates before coming to an end at a point where a track leads up from the valley on the left.

Walk along the ledge which curves to the right until it joins the track and then follow the track straight ahead. It goes through a gateway beyond which a narrow path leads away to the left. Ignore this and continue along the track which goes up a slope.

Near the top of the slope the track branches. Keep to the left fork which leads straight ahead. As the track curves to the right, leave it and go straight on along a faint grassy path.

At the top of the hill this path joins another from the right and leads to a gate. Go through the gate and follow the track beyond. After some distance it merges with a track from the right and runs down a slope to a gate with a stile beside it. Go through the gate and follow the track on along the ridge. This will eventually give you a good view of Corfe Castle straight ahead.

Where the track curves sharply to the left and another path leads straight on, turn right to follow the field fence down the slope. This will bring you to a narrow path which leads down to a gate. Go through the gate and follow the track through the trees. It is joined by another from the right and then leads on down the slope to the place where you left the car.

Walk 7   Badbury Rings

4 miles (6 km)

OS sheet 195
Start: Badbury Rings car park

Badbury Rings is an Iron Age hill-fort protected by three concentric sets of ramparts and ditches. It commands a view which stretches from the Purbeck hills in the west to Cranborne Chase in the east and was once an important tribal stronghold. Legend has it that it was the Mount Badon where King Arthur defeated the Saxons.

The beech avenue lines the road to Blandford which runs past the west side of Badbury Rings. It was planted over a hundred years ago and stretches for two miles from the gates of Kingston Lacy park to what used to be the edge of Kingston Lacy estate.

The avenue is said to have been set out so that the number of trees on one side represented the days in a year and those on the other the days in a leap year. If this was the original intention it is certainly no longer the case.

Take the B3082 that runs from Wimborne to Blandford. This is the road on which the beech avenue is situated. Just over half-way along the avenue a green signpost indicates the entrance to Badbury Rings. The turning to Badbury Rings gives access to a well defined track which leads up a slight slope to a large parking area beside the earthwork.

Walk round the hill-fort in an anti-clockwise direction. This will take you across the top of the wide expanse of grass which divides the rings from the road and will eventually bring you to a place where the outer rampart meets a hedge.

Just before this point a grassy track leads down the slope to the right. Follow it until it bends sharply to the right beside the beech avenue. Here it is joined by another less distinct track from the left, although the junction is partly blocked by mounds of earth. Turn left and cross these obstructions keeping the trees of the beech avenue on your right.

Within a short distance you will pass a place where another track leads away to the left. Disregard this and carry straight on until you reach the end of the beech avenue and see the gates and lodge of Kingston Lacy park on the opposite side of the road. Here the track also comes to an end as it meets another in a T-junction. Cross the head of

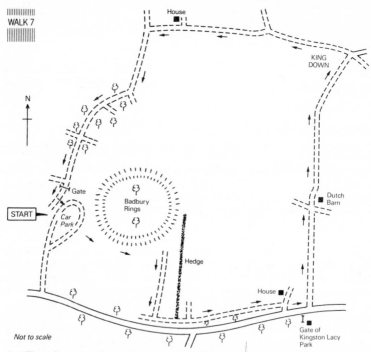

the T and go on along the verge for about a hundred yards until you reach a second track marked 'Bridleway Bradford Barrow $1\frac{1}{2}$', then turn left.

After some distance you will come to a place near a Dutch barn where four tracks meet. Take the one that leads straight ahead passing the barn on the right. The track winds between fields and eventually ends in a junction where there is a lane and a track to the right and another track to the left. Take the left-hand track which leads down a slope and then forks. Keep left following the branch that goes more or less straight ahead up the next slight hill.

On the far side of the hill the track dips down towards a white house beside which it is joined by another track from the right. Ignore this and carry straight on passing the house on your right.

Not far from the house, at a point where it is joined by a grassy track from the right, the track turns sharp left and climbs a hill. At the top of the slope it comes to a wood. A secondary track leads away to the right through the trees. Turn sharp right to follow this. Having passed a turning to the left marked private, it will bring you to a place where two paths cross. Go straight ahead and within a very short distance you will emerge from the trees.

Continue to follow the track as it leads down a hill and passes through a gateway on to the open grassland surrounding Badbury Rings. The car park is now straight ahead at the top of the slope.

30

Walk 8   Worth Matravers

5½ miles (8·5 km)

OS sheet 181
Start: Worth Matravers car park

Worth Matravers is one of the most beautiful of the Purbeck villages. It is an old quarrymen's village and the famous Purbeck stone has been quarried here since Norman times. The lovely grey stone cottages and the ancient church are built of it and the hills around the village are honeycombed with quarries; some still in use and others, like those at Winspit, deserted long ago.

St Aldhelm's Chapel, which stands on the cliff at St Aldhelm's Head, is a quaint little Norman building named after a local saint who became the first Saxon Bishop of Sherborne. During Norman times a priest lived a lonely life here combining his religious duties with those of a coastguard.

From the cliff top beyond St Aldhelm's Chapel one of the most beautiful views of the Dorset coast is to be seen. Bird life abounds here and, for those who are feeling energetic, a narrow path leads down to another local beauty spot, Chapman's Pool.

For the purpose of parking it is best to approach Worth Matravers from the turning on the B3069, Kingston to Langton Matravers road, known as Worth Gate. This is the first turning on the right coming from Kingston. Follow the road from Worth Gate to Worth Matravers and just as you enter the outskirts of the village there is a car park on the right.

Turn right out of the car park and follow the road down the hill bearing right at the junction by The Square and Compass public house. Where the road turns sharp right near the bottom of the hill cross over and carry on down, keeping the duck pond on your right. Follow the lane as it curves to the right then take the second turning on the left.

This is a very short cul-de-sac and in the left-hand corner at the end there is a stile with a small gate beside it. Go over the stile and follow the footpath down the hill over two more stiles. After the third stile the path widens and within a hundred yards joins another wide track in a T-junction with a small water gauging station on the right-hand side. Turn left and follow this track down through the valley.

After about a quarter of a mile a gate bars the way but, should this be locked, there is a stone stile beside it. Cross this and continue to

31

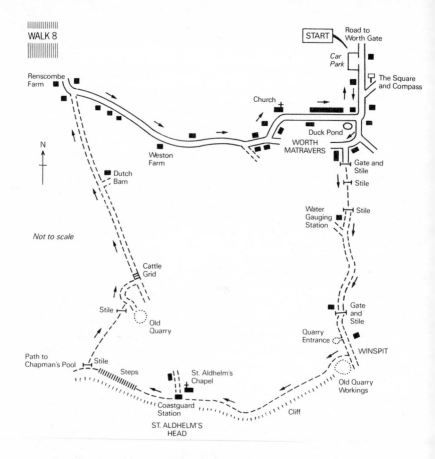

follow the main track. Before long it will curve to the left. A small cottage nestles in the valley on your left, and directly opposite, on the right, is an old quarry entrance sealed off with a grating. Just beyond this on the right the fence comes to an end and a narrow path marked 'To St Aldhelm's Head' leads up to the cliff top.

The first part of this path is steep but it is a short climb and at the top the walker is rewarded by a magnificent view down across the old quarry workings to the tiny inlet of Winspit from where the coastline curves round to the lighthouse near Durlston Head.

Follow the path along the cliff top. It is fairly narrow but easy walking and quite safe provided you remember to keep well away from the edge. After about a mile the fence which borders the path turns inland and the path forks. Take either branch, they both lead up the short slope and join again at the top where you will see St Aldhelm's Chapel and the coastguard station straight ahead of you.

It is well worth pausing a while to visit the tiny chapel which is an almost unique survival of a series of similar buildings that once served as landmarks and lookout posts along our coasts. Then, from the coastguard station, continue along the cliff path which is marked at this point 'To Chapman's Pool $1\frac{1}{4}$ miles'.

Within a hundred yards you will come to a flight of steps cut into the side of the hill. The view from the top is breath-taking and must be one of the best to be seen on the whole of the Dorset coast.

Descend the steps and turn right across the stile into the field. Walk up through the valley and leave the field by another stile at the far end. Slightly to the right is a track which leads up the hill from a quarry. Follow it to the top and when it joins the track on the hill crest turn left. There is a cattle grid across the hill-top track at this point but it is so engulfed in earth that it is almost unnoticeable and certainly no hindrance to easy walking.

About a quarter of a mile further on, to the right by a Dutch barn, there is another track marked 'Worth $\frac{3}{4}$. No cars'. This can serve as a short cut for it brings you out just west of the village but its surface is uneven and the initial part can become very muddy in wet weather. It is best to ignore it and carry straight on to Renscombe Farm.

At the farm the track joins the lane to Chapman's Pool. Turn right and follow the lane. It will lead you past a group of bungalows and Weston Farm on the right to the outskirts of Worth Matravers.

Continue to follow the road through the village bearing round to the left towards the church. If you have time pause to give it a closer inspection for this is a fine building and one of the oldest churches in Dorset.

Beyond the church the road slopes down the hill. At the bottom the duck pond is on your right. Turn left and go up the hill keeping The Square and Compass on your right. This will bring you back to the car park.

4½ miles (7 km)

OS sheet 195
Start: Cocknowle

The Isle of Purbeck is one of the most beautiful parts of the county of Dorset. It is a place of softly rolling hills, picturesque grey stone villages and magnificent views. The beginning and end of this walk give you the opportunity to enjoy some of the best of these views. Both sections cover the same piece of ground: a ridge from which, in the outward direction, the walker can see the wide expanse of water that is known as Poole Harbour. This is the second largest natural harbour in the world. It is dotted with densely wooded islands and bordered on the Purbeck side by open heathland. On the far shore the ancient port of Poole and the town of Bournemouth are to be seen on the horizon.

The return journey along the ridge affords the walker equally good views in the opposite direction. This time the panorama takes in the village of Church Knowle and the hills around Swyre Head with the sea in the distance.

Corfe Castle is one of the most beautiful of the Purbeck villages; a place steeped in history and tradition and dominated by the ruins of its ancient castle. It is in the streets of Corfe Castle that the quarrymen play their famous game of football every Shrove Tuesday. This game consists of kicking a ball right round the village. It is the surviving remnant of a custom that once ensured the quarrymen access to the quays from which the Purbeck stone was shipped.

The castle was built by the Normans to protect the entrance to Purbeck. It was once a royal castle and gained an evil reputation during the Middle Ages when its dungeons served as a convenient prison for those unfortunate enough to have incurred the king's displeasure.

During the seventeenth century, when England was torn by civil war, the castle was heroically defended by Lady Mary Bankes and a small group of retainers against the might of the Roundhead army. The strength of the castle was so great that, even with such a small band of people to defend it, the first attack was repulsed. In fact it is possible that the castle would never have been defeated had not one of the garrison treacherously surrendered it when the Parliamentarians returned some time later.

Having gained control of the castle Parliament ordered that it should be destroyed. It was decided that the best way to do this was to blow it up but, although virtually all the gunpowder available in

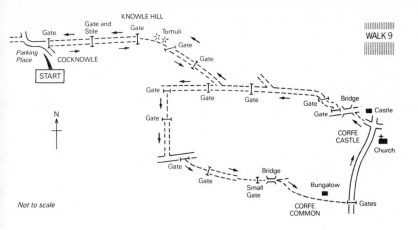

Dorset was used, the Norman builders had done their work so well that the attempt was only partly successful. Instead of reducing the castle to a heap of rubble, enough of the outer walls and the keep remained for present day visitors to be able to gain a good idea of what an impressive building the castle must once have been.

Take the A351 from Wareham travelling towards Swanage. At the outskirts of Corfe Castle turn right on to the road to Church Knowle, Steeple and Kimmeridge. Having passed through Church Knowle village turn right again at the crossroads on to a narrow lane sign-posted 'Stoborough 3½ Wareham 4¼'. The lane climbs a hill between high banks, passing the cottages which make up the tiny hamlet of Cocknowle. The road turns left, slightly left again and then sharp right at the top of the slope. At this point a track leads straight ahead and it is possible to park on the left near where it leaves the road.

Go back down the hill for a short distance to take a track marked 'Bridleway Corfe Castle 1¾' which leads straight up the hill through a gate to the left. Follow the track on along the ridge passing Church Knowle in the valley below.

This will bring you to another gate with a stile beside it. Cross the stile and carry straight on to reach a gate at the far side of the field. From here take the narrow path which veers slightly to the right across the hillside.

The path passes two tumuli on the left and then leads to a gate in the fence to the right. Beyond this take the track which goes down the hill passing through a second gate to reach the valley. Here the track merges with another which comes through a gate to the right.

Turn right on to this and follow it until you come to a place where the fence on the left sweeps round to accommodate a water trough in the hedge. At the point where it rejoins the track there is a metal gate on the left. Go through this and follow the hedge on the left to a second gate in the bottom left-hand corner of the field. This gives access to a track which leads to the road.

Turn left and walk along the road for about a hundred yards to reach a gate on the right marked 'Bridleway'. Go through the gate and walk obliquely left across the field to reach another gate with a track beyond it. As the track crosses the field it slowly becomes fainter and eventually fades altogether. Carry straight on and go down a slight slope to reach a U-shaped extension in the far corner of the field.

Leave the field by a small gate half hidden amongst the bushes in the right-hand corner of this extension. Beyond it the path leads over a small humpbacked bridge and then divides. Take the right-hand fork which goes up the slope.

The path winds its way through a group of bushes and then passes a bungalow on the left to reach a semicircle of gates which give access to the road. Turn left to follow the road down through the village.

The far end of this road is part of the route used by the quarrymen for their Shrove Tuesday football game. This traditionally begins at the Fox Inn which is on the left opposite the church.

Having passed the church the road turns to the right, but ignore this and go straight on towards the castle entrance. Turn left beside a café called The Old Tea House and, at the end of the short cul-de-sac, right on to a path which skirts the castle mound.

When the path emerges on to the road turn left. Cross the bridge and turn right to go through a gate marked 'Bridleway Bare Cross $1\frac{3}{4}$'.

On the far side of the gate bear left to follow the track which leads up a slight slope and curves to the right to reach a second gate. Go through this and carry on along the track. Where it forks take the left-hand branch which continues up the slope to another gate.

Some distance beyond this gate the track forks again. This time take the right-hand branch which is the one you originally came down.

Follow it up the slope passing through the two gates to reach the narrow path. Retrace your steps along this and across the field beyond to reach the track which leads along the ridge to the road where you left the car.

Walk 10   Houns-tout and Chapman's Pool

$3\frac{1}{2}$ miles (5.5 km)

OS sheet 195
Start: car park near Kingston

The village of Kingston stands high on the ridge of the Purbeck hills. It has two churches, the elder disused and the younger an impressive, nineteenth-century building which looks more like a miniature cathedral than a village church. From the village street there are fine views across the valley towards Corfe Castle.

Houns-tout cliff, which guards the western side of Chapman's Pool, is approached along a ridge overlooking the Encombe Estate. This was once owned by the 1st Earl of Eldon who was William Pitt's Lord Chancellor. The views across the estate from the ridge are quite magnificent and include an obelisk erected to the memory of Lord Eldon's brother, Lord Stowell.

From Houns-tout Cliff itself there are good views of Chapman's Pool. This is a completely unspoilt part of the Dorset coast and very beautiful.

Take the B3069 from Corfe Castle heading towards Langton Matravers. At the top of the hill which leads up to Kingston turn right beside the Scott Arms. Follow the road straight ahead. Having left the village behind, the car park for Houns-tout is on the left.

Leave the car park by the narrow path through the bushes. This is beside the notice board at the rear of the parking area.

Where the path joins an unmetalled track turn right. The track runs for some distance between belts of trees, swings right then left and is joined by two tracks from the right and one from the left. Ignore these and carry straight on to where the track divides. Keep to the left-hand fork which, within a short distance, divides again. This time take the right-hand fork. It leads to a field gate with a stile beside it.

Cross the stile and go straight ahead following the wall on the left. At this point the obelisk erected to the memory of Lord Stowell is to be seen on the hillside to the right.

Eventually you will come to another gate and stile, beyond which keep to the track that follows the wall. After a while this track is joined by another which comes up the hillside from the right. Disregard this and carry straight on along the ridge passing through another gate with a stile beside it.

Cross the stile at the end of the ridge and follow the narrow path to a

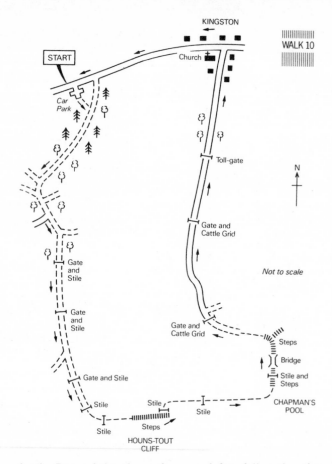

KINGSTON

START

Church

Car Park

Toll-gate

Gate and Cattle Grid

N

Not to scale

Gate and Stile

Gate and Stile

Gate and Stile

Gate and Cattle Grid

Steps

Bridge

Stile and Steps

CHAPMAN'S POOL

Stile

Stile

Stile

Stile

Steps

HOUNS-TOUT CLIFF

second stile. Beyond this the path curves left to follow the edge of the cliff to the top of a flight of steps. At this point there are good views of Chapman's Pool in the valley below.

Go down the steps and turn sharp left to cross a stile; then turn right to follow the path down the hillside to another stile. Cross this and continue along the path which skirts the fence. The path then turns left to descend another shorter flight of steps intersected by a stile.

At the bottom of the slope the path crosses a small bridge and is joined by another path from the right. Ignore this and go up the steps straight ahead.

Near the top the path forks. Take the left-hand fork which ascends three more steps and then goes straight ahead to join a track. This leads to a cattle grid with a gate beside it. Go through the gate and follow the metalled lane straight ahead disregarding a track which leads away to the right.

The lane goes up a hill and crosses another cattle grid. Beyond this it goes on for some distance before leading through the toll-gate and on to Kingston village. Having passed the younger of the village's two churches on the left, the lane joins the road in a T-junction. Turn left and follow the road back to the car park.

Walk 11   Ashmore

3 miles (4·5 km)

OS sheet 184
Start: Ashmore

The village of Ashmore gains its title from the beautiful pond which lies at its heart, for the name Ashmore is derived from Asshemere, 'the lake by the ash trees'. This pond was once a very important stretch of water. It lay on one of the ancient trackways known as the Great Ridgeway and it very rarely dried up. Today it is just a pond. It is surrounded by pretty cottages and old farm buildings and is the home of a large collection of ducks.

Yet it is not just the pond which makes this part of the county well worth a visit. Ashmore is 700 ft above sea-level. It is the highest village in Dorset and from the surrounding country it is possible to see as far as the Isle of Wight and Purbeck.

Parts of this walk lead through pleasant woods where the timid woodland birds and animals are to be seen. The trees are deciduous and in autumn add a riot of colour to already delightful surroundings.

Take the A350 from Blandford travelling towards Shaftesbury and turn right in Fontmell Magna to follow the road signs to Ashmore. Drive through the village to the pond and park by the war memorial on the left.

Go back through the village. Having passed the church on your right and four garages on your left, turn left on to a gravel track marked 'Bridleway only No motors'. This track runs through open fields along the top of the hill and gives excellent views.

Carry on along the track until you come to a belt of trees on the right-hand side. Beyond these a track leads away to the right passing a Dutch barn on the left. Walk along this track to where it ends at a field gate. Beside the gate turn right to go through a second gate which gives access to a grassy track.

Follow this track through the trees. It goes down a slope and is crossed by another track. Turn left on to this passing a large horse chestnut tree on the right. The track quickly degenerates into a path. At intervals it is joined by grassy tracks from the right but ignore these and carry straight on to where the track joins another which comes down a slope to the left.

Go straight ahead following the track through the trees until you reach a place where it joins a wider track in a T-junction with a

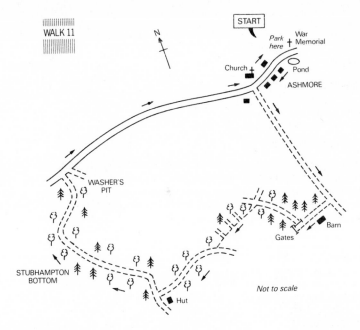

WALK 11

START

Park here

War Memorial

Church

Pond

ASHMORE

N

WASHER'S PIT

Barn

Gates

STUBHAMPTON BOTTOM

Hut

Not to scale

corrugated iron hut on the left-hand side. This is Stubhampton Bottom.

Turn right on to the wide track and follow it until you eventually come to the road at Washers Pit. Turn right and walk along the road which leads up a hill to the village. Carry straight on passing the church on the left to reach the place where you left the car.

Walk 12   Tarrant Crawford

5 miles (8 km)

OS sheet 195
Start: Tarrant Keyneston

Tarrant Keyneston and Tarrant Crawford get their names from the
little River Tarrant which flows down through the hills from Cranborne Chase to join the River Stour near Spetisbury. Tarrant
Keyneston is a fairly large village with a few pretty thatched cottages
but Tarrant Crawford consists of little more than a church and a
farm. Yet in the past Tarrant Crawford was the more important of the
two. There was once a Cistercian abbey here although today little
remains of it except a few green mounds near the church.

Bishop Poore, the founder of Salisbury Cathedral, was born in
Tarrant Crawford. He was instrumental in founding the abbey and it
is thought that he wrote one of the finest books ever written in Middle
English, the *Ancren Riwle* or the Nun's Rule, for its earliest
inhabitants.

Bishop Poore was one of the two important people to be buried in
the nunnery. The other was Queen Joan of Scotland who was a
daughter of King John. Both their graves are lost beneath the grass
which covers the abbey ruins but beside the altar in the church are
two coffin lids which are said to have come from them.

Spettisbury Rings is an ancient earthwork on the top of the hill
overlooking Spetisbury village. It was originally an Iron Age
stronghold but was later used by the Saxons.

Crawford Bridge is an old, nine-arched bridge which spans the
River Stour. It was restored in 1500 but was built almost a century
earlier.

Take the B3082 from Wimborne travelling towards Blandford and
turn left opposite the True Lover's Knot public house in Tarrant
Keyneston on to the road to Tarrant Crawford. Drive through
Tarrant Keyneston village. Just after passing the church on the right
the road swings to the right. Park on the left at this point beside a path
marked 'Bridleway Tarrant Crawford ¾'.

Walk down the path to where it joins a track then follow the track
straight ahead keeping the little River Tarrant on the right. This will
lead you past Tarrant Crawford church on the left.

Just beyond the church there are some farm buildings on the right.
Opposite them turn left through a field gate to follow a track which

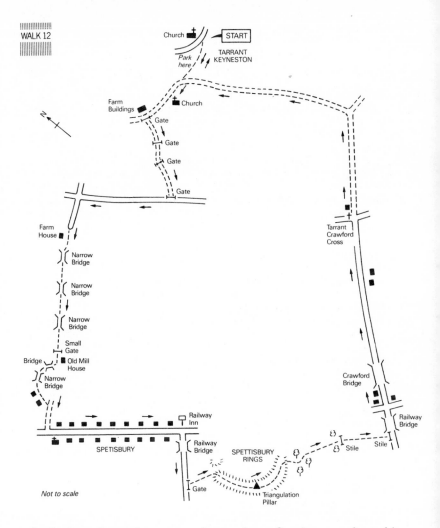

Church   START

TARRANT KEYNESTON

Park here

Farm Buildings   Church

Gate

Gate

Gate

Gate

Farm House

Narrow Bridge

Narrow Bridge

Narrow Bridge

Small Gate

Bridge   Old Mill House

Narrow Bridge

Railway Inn

Railway Bridge

SPETISBURY

SPETTISBURY RINGS

Gate

Triangulation Pillar

Stile

Stile

Crawford Bridge

Railway Bridge

Tarrant Crawford Cross

Not to scale

leads through another gate and up a slope. Continue on along this track until you come to the road and then turn right.

Follow the road to the crossroads and turn left on to the road to Keynston Mill. This road leads down to a farm. Pass in front of the farmhouse and then carry straight on to cross the river by a narrow bridge. At the far side of this go straight ahead crossing the meadows by a path which goes over two more narrow bridges.

After the second of these bridges head for a small gate in the top right-hand corner of the field. This gives access to a path which goes past the Old Mill House. Beside the house the path turns right to

43

cross an old bridge. From the top of this the remains of the mill-race are to be seen on the right.

Having crossed the bridge turn left across another narrow bridge to take a path which leads past some cottages on the right to a track. Turn right and follow the track up to the road.

At the road turn left and walk on until you come to the Railway Inn on the left. Cross the road and follow the lane which leads up under the railway bridge. Beyond the bridge go on up the hill and turn left through a field gate on to a footpath marked 'Spettisbury Ring & Middle Buildings $\frac{3}{4}$'.

Go up the slope to the earthwork and at the entrance turn right on to the top of the rampart. Walk round this to the triangulation pillar from which there are good views across the valley, and then carry on to where some hawthorn bushes partly obstruct the path. Just before them turn right on to a narrow path which leads down to the ditch on the outside of the rampart. Cross the ditch and go through the trees to the field.

Walk diagonally left across the field to where a path goes through some bushes to a stile. Cross the stile and walk along the edge of the field to where a second stile gives access to the lane.

Turn left and follow the lane down under the railway bridge to the main road. Cross this and follow the road straight ahead. This will lead you over Crawford Bridge and up to the T-junction where the remains of the old Tarrant Crawford cross stand in the middle of the road. At this point go straight ahead to follow a gravel track which leads between the fields. It is signposted 'Bridleway to Witchampton $4\frac{3}{4}$'.

Where the track forks take the left-hand branch. Follow it until it swings left beside the River Tarrant then turn right on to the path which leads back to the car.

Walk 13   Ibberton Hill and Turnworth

6½ miles (10 km)

OS sheet 194
Start: Ibberton Hill picnic site

This walk can be recommended mainly for its views. Ibberton Hill is a well known Dorset beauty spot. It is one of the highest hills in the county and on a clear day the view to the north-east extends well into Somerset.

From Okeford Hill the walker is afforded a magnificent view of Hambledon Hill. It is crowned with an Iron Age hill-fort which had its beginnings in Neolithic times.

Take the A357 which runs from Durweston to Sturminster Newton and turn left in Shillingstone to follow the signs for Ibberton and Bulbarrow. At the top of Ibberton Hill there is a picnic site on the left. It is a wide expanse of grass with plenty of room for parking.

Leave the picnic site and follow the road back in the direction from which you came. After passing a turning to Ibberton it goes up a slight rise and bends to the left. At this point a gravel track joins the road on the right. It is marked 'Footpath Okeford Hill 1½ miles'. Take this track. It branches almost immediately, as a bridleway to Turnworth leads through a gateway on the right, but ignore this and carry straight on.

After about 150 yards the track forks again. Keep to the left-hand branch which follows the ridge and eventually crosses the Turnworth road on the crest of Okeford Hill. Cross the road and carry on along the track which leads up a slope towards a wood. After about a hundred yards a second track leads through a gate to the right. Disregard this and go straight on keeping the Forestry Commission sign marked 'Wareham Forest, Okeford Hill' on the right.

Within a very short distance the track forks to the left. Take the right-hand branch which leads straight ahead and is partly obstructed by a vehicle barrier. As the track emerges from the trees another track leads steeply down the hill to the left giving a good view across the valley of the Stour to Hambledon Hill. Although it is well worth pausing to admire the view do not turn left. Keep straight on along the track which runs between a stand of trees on the left and a fence on the right. Where the track divides take the right-hand fork which leads through a gateway and passes a triangulation pillar on the right.

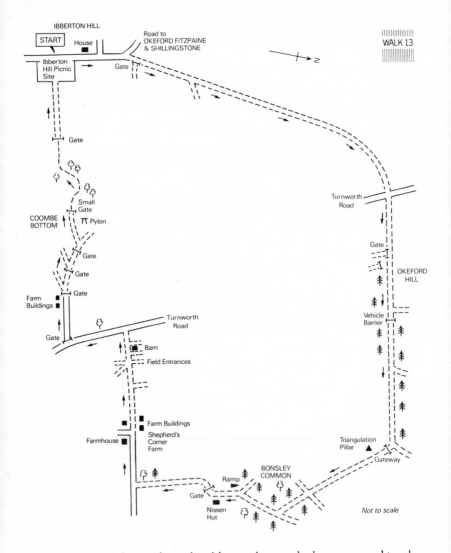

Keep straight on along the ridge to the wood where a second track crosses the first at right-angles. Ignore this and carry straight on to where the track meets another in a T-junction. Turn right and follow this track through the trees.

After about a hundred yards it bears to the left at a point where another track joins it from the right by a concrete ramp. Keep left passing a Nissen hut on the left. The track curves to the right passing through a gateway then left again to follow the hedge. Eventually, having passed another small wood on the right, it emerges on to a lane.

Turn right and follow the lane down the hill to the farm. Here it curves sharply left and a track leads straight ahead between the farm buildings. Leave the lane to follow this track up the hill. On the crest it is joined by another track from the right. Ignore this and carry straight on down the slope passing a junction with some field gates and a barn on the right to reach the Turnworth road.

Turn left to follow the road. After about 350 yards swing right on to a metalled lane which leads through a pair of gates and up a slope. Continue on along this lane passing some farm buildings on the left.

At this point the lane degenerates into a gravel track which goes through another pair of gates and then forks. Keep to the right-hand fork which runs on through the valley beside the fence.

After passing through a third pair of gates the track forks again. Keep to the right-hand branch which curves to the right and passes through yet another pair of gates. Just beyond these, turn left to take the track which follows the fence up the hill towards the electricity pylon. Here the track leaves the fence and carries on up the slope towards a little wood.

Near the top of the hill the track ends at a fence in which there is a wire gate with a small metal gate beside it. Go through the small gate and follow the fence on the right. This leads past the wood and then on towards a second wood.

Carry on along the side of the second wood to where the fence turns sharp right to descend the slope. At this point leave the fence and go straight ahead passing a solitary oak tree on your left to reach a track that comes through the hedge at the far side of the field. This leads back to Ibberton Hill picnic site.

Walk 14   Milton Abbas

2 miles (3 km)

OS sheet 194
Start: Milton Abbas

Milton Abbas is a very picturesque village with a unique history. In 1771 Lord Milton, 1st Earl of Dorchester, had a beautiful mansion built beside the old abbey church in the market town of Milton Abbas. In spite of its situation he wished his house to be set in spacious grounds so he ruthlessly obliterated the whole of Milton Abbas town to make way for a large park. He rehoused the townsfolk in a new model village which he built on the curving slope of the Blandford road out of sight of his house.

Milton Abbey was founded in 932 by King Athelstan as a college of canons and later became a Benedictine monastery. The original abbey church was destroyed by fire at the beginning of the fourteenth century and was never fully rebuilt. It has no nave because the Dissolution of the Monasteries came before it was completed.

After the Dissolution of the Monasteries the abbey and its property was bought by Sir John Tregonwell. It was one of his descendants, another John Tregonwell, who had a very narrow escape there during the next century when he fell from the top of the abbey church's tower. He was only five years old and had been taken to the top of the tower by his nurse. Whilst leaning over the parapet to pick a wild rose he slipped and fell. His nurse fled back down the stairs in a panic only to find her charge unconcernedly collecting daisies on the grass below. He had been saved from injury by his nankeen petticoat which had acted as a parachute and floated him safely down to earth.

St Catherine's Chapel stands high on the hill overlooking the abbey church to which it is connected by a flight of grassy steps. The chapel is over 800 years old and was originally built as a wayfarer's chapel where travellers and pilgrims could pause to pray.

During the nineteenth century the chapel was used as a pigeon house. It was later converted into a labourer's cottage, a carpenter's workshop and then a timber store. It was restored to its original use in 1901 by Everard Hambro who owned the estate at the time. Today the chapel, which is regularly used, is maintained by the boys of Milton Abbey School together with a few dedicated parishioners.

Take the A354 from Blandford travelling towards Puddletown and turn right in Winterborne Whitechurch on to the road to Milton

48

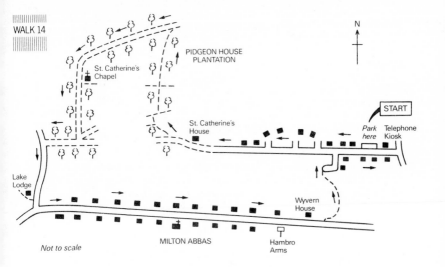

Abbas and Bulbarrow. After about two and a half miles you will come
to a turning on the left signposted Milton Abbas. Pass this and take
the next turning on the left by the bus shelter. Park on the right in the
parking spaces by the telephone kiosk.

Walk straight on along the road passing the council houses on your
right. Just beyond them the road degenerates into an unmetalled
lane. Continue along this until you pass St Catherine's House on the
right. The lane then leads down a hill through some trees.

Just as it enters the trees a path leads away to the right. Turn on to
this and where it forks take the right-hand branch which leads up a
short sharp slope and joins a wider path. Turn right and then almost
immediately left on to another path which leads straight ahead
through the trees.

After some distance the path is crossed by another. Ignore this and
carry straight on until the path swings right to join a track. Turn
sharp left to follow this track which curves to the left to pass St.
Catherine's Chapel.

At the point where the path passes the chapel there is a magnificent
view of Milton Abbey in the valley to the right. Part of Lord Milton's
house, which is now a public school, is also just visible beside it. A
bench has been thoughtfully provided against the chapel wall so that
walkers can rest and one or other of the chapel doors is generally left
open for visitors who wish to study the interior of the building.

On leaving the chapel carry straight on along the track ignoring a
path which leads up the hill to the left. When you reach the place
where the track meets an unmetalled lane turn right and walk down
the hill to the road.

Turn left and follow the road to the T-junction. Just before

49

reaching it there is a cottage on the right called Lake Lodge. Beside it a path leads through some gates. This is a public footpath to Milton Abbey and makes a worthwhile diversion for those who would like a closer look at this fine old church.

At the T-junction turn left to walk up through Milton Abbas village. The view of the village from just beyond the junction is probably the very best to be obtained.

Carry straight on up the hill, passing the Hambro Arms on the right, to where the left-hand pavement ends outside Wyvern House. Not far beyond this a footpath leads away to the left. Turn on to this and follow it up the slope to where it emerges at the head of a cul-de-sac. Follow the cul-de-sac round to the left and where it joins the road turn right to walk back to the car.

Walk 15   Lulworth Cove and Durdle Door

3 miles (4·5 km)

OS sheet 194
Start: Lulworth Cove car park

Lulworth Cove is one of the most famous beauty spots on the Dorset coast. It is a small circular bay enclosed within a wall of steep cliffs and bordered by a shingle beach. A narrow road runs down to the beach through West Lulworth village which possesses many pleasant old cottages. Once solely a fishing village West Lulworth now gains a larger income from its tourist trade. It has been a popular place with holiday-makers for well over a hundred years and amongst its more distinguished visitors were Rupert Brooke and John Keats. The latter spent his last day in England here and also wrote his last sonnet whilst visiting the village.

Durdle Door is an impressive natural arch of Portland stone which stands in the sea to the west of Lulworth Cove. It is joined to the mainland by a narrow isthmus and divides the section of coast west of Lulworth into two pleasant beaches.

The coastal scenery around Lulworth Cove is some of the most beautiful in Dorset. Here the high chalk hills meet the sea and the white cliffs which mark their end provide spectacular views.

Take the A352 from Wareham travelling towards Weymouth and, having crossed the railway line at Wool, turn left on to the B3071 to Lulworth Cove. Park in the main car park for Lulworth Cove, which is almost at the far end of West Lulworth village on the right.

Walk up the track to the pair of gates at the far end of the car park. Go through the smaller of the two and turn sharp right to follow the fence. Where the fence bends to the left there is a stile on the right, but ignore this and continue to follow the fence. This will eventually bring you to another stile straight ahead of you. Cross this and continue to follow the fence on the right up the slope. At the top bear slightly left to go through a gateway with a stile beside it. Beyond the gateway turn right on to a metalled lane which leads through a caravan site. As the lane leaves the caravan site and climbs up a slope towards the road a footpath runs beside it on the left. Take this footpath and at the top of the slope follow it round to the left towards the farmhouse.

Where the footpath ends turn right on to a track which goes round the side of the farm building on the right. Within a very short distance a second track leads away to the left. Turn on to this and follow it

51

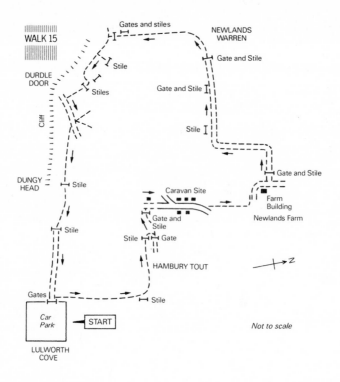

through a gate with a stile beside it. The track goes straight on for some distance before swinging left to descend a slope towards the holiday camp.

At the bottom of the slope turn right to follow the fence on the left. This will lead you past a stile and then a gate with a stile beside it. Ignore both of these and carry on down the slope to where the fence on the left ends and a gate and stile give access to a grassy path straight ahead.

Take this path, which curves left following the course of the valley and eventually ends at a point where there is a gate and a stile straight ahead and another on the right. Go over the stile straight ahead and then turn slightly left to follow a narrow grassy path which skirts the cliff.

Ignore a path which leads away to a stile set on the hillside to the left and continue to follow the one along the top of the cliff, in this way you will gain a good view of Durdle Door before the path swings slightly left and leads to a place where there are two stiles. One of these stiles gives access to the upper slopes of the hill, the other is situated on a path which leads down a slope to a track on the cliff top. Cross this second stile and walk down to the track. Turn left and follow the track to where it leaves the cliff and starts to climb the hill. At this point a grassy path continues to follow the edge of the cliff.

Leave the track to take the path which will eventually bring you to a stile at a place where a track leads away to the right. Disregard this track and cross the stile to follow the path straight ahead. This will bring you to a second stile from which there are beautiful views of Lulworth Cove in the valley straight ahead.

Cross the second stile and follow the track which leads down the hillside to the gates which give access to the car park.

Walk 16   Hilton

4½ miles (7 km)

OS sheet 194
Start: Bulbarrow Hill

Bulbarrow Hill, the summit of which is over 900 ft above sea level, is the second highe t hill in Dorset. It is surmounted by a radio mast which can be seen for miles around and is part of the chalk uplands which stretch into Dorset from Wiltshire. The area surrounding Bulbarrow is farmland which has a remote grandeur all of its own, and affords the walker the opportunity of enjoying some of the Dorset countryside at its best.

Hilton, in spite of its name, nestles in the valley below Bulbarrow. It is a pleasant little village with several thatched cottages and a fine fifteenth-century church.

On the top of Green Hill which is to the north of Milton Abbas there is a small nature reserve. It is called the Green Hill Down Reserve and is run by the Dorset Naturalists' Trust in conjunction with the owner Mrs. Hughes.

Take the A354 from Blandford travelling towards Puddletown and turn right in Winterborne Whitechurch to follow the signs to Bulbarrow. After five and a half miles you will come to a road junction on the crest of Woolland Hill. Turn left on to the road to Ansty and Hilton. Having passed two radio masts on the right the road begins to slope downhill. Follow it for approximately another hundred yards and, just before it swings left, park on the left-hand verge beside two beech trees.

Walk on along the road for a short distance and then turn left on to a track marked 'Bridleway Hilton and Milton Abbey'. This leads through a gate, skirts a hedge on the left and eventually widens at a place where there are three gates; one straight ahead and the others on either side. Go through the one straight ahead and continue along the track.

Within a very short distance the track forks. Take the right-hand branch which leads obliquely down the hill passing a wood on the right. The track then forks again but this time take either fork for they both swing left and rejoin within a very short distance before leading down the hill towards a barn in the valley.

Go through the gate at the bottom of the slope and bear left to pass the barn on your right. Ignoring the track which leads more or less

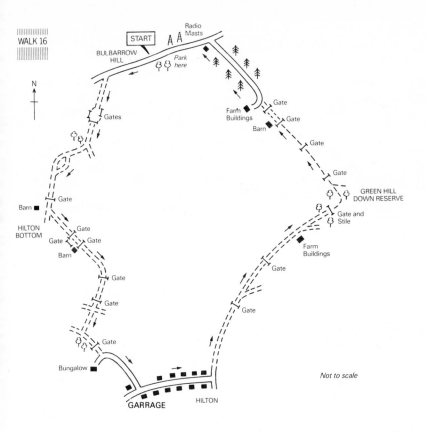

WALK 16

START

Radio Masts

BULBARROW HILL

Park here

N

Gates

Farm Buildings

Gate
Gate

Barn

Gate

Gate

Gate

GREEN HILL DOWN RESERVE

Gate and Stile

Gate

Barn

HILTON BOTTOM

Gate

Gate

Gate

Gate

Barn

Farm Buildings

Gate

Gate

Gate

Gate

Bungalow

GARRAGE

HILTON

Not to scale

straight ahead, turn left to follow a second which leads towards another barn behind the hedge at the far side of the field. From here your route continues along the track but if it is muddy beside the barn turn sharp right through a gateway and go round behind the barn to rejoin the track on the far side.

Having crossed the field the track swings right through a gate. Follow it to a second gate and beyond this carry straight on ignoring a track which leads up to the farm on the right.

Within a short distance the track you are following merges with another. Turn left on to this and follow it through a gate to where it joins a metalled track which leads down from a bungalow on the right. Carry straight on along the metalled track which goes through a gate and eventually joins a lane in a T-junction. Turn left and follow the lane until you come to another T-junction then turn left again.

This branch of the lane almost immediately degenerates into a track which leads up a slope between hedges. After a while the hedge to the right comes to an end and the track passes through a gateway.

55

Continue to follow it up the slope keeping to the left where it forks until you come to a second gate. Go through this and straight on until you come to some derelict farm buildings on the right. Here the track forks. Take the branch which leads straight ahead. It passes through a grove of trees to reach a gate with a stile beside it. This is the entrance to Green Hill Down Reserve.

Go through the gate and turn left to skirt a patch of brambles on the left and take a narrow path which leads through the bushes. After a short distance this is joined by another path from the right but ignore this and carry straight on until you reach a gate. Go through this and follow the fence on the left passing through a gate at the far side of the field and continuing until you reach another gate at the end of the second field. This opens on to a track which goes straight ahead passing a barn on the left. It then leads through a gate and joins a metalled track which swings round from some farm buildings on the left. Follow this track straight ahead through the trees until it reaches the road. Turn left and walk back along the road to the car.

Walk 17   Ringstead Bay and Durdle Door

8 miles (12·5 km)

OS sheet 194
Start: Daggers Gate

The tall grassy hills which end in the precipitous cliffs at Swyre Head, Bat's Head and White Nothe make part of the latter half of this walk into a series of steep ascents and descents and, although the cliff path is quite safe, this is not a walk for people who suffer from vertigo. However, for those who are fairly energetic and enjoy magnificent scenery it is not to be surpassed. The coastline between Durdle Door and Ringstead Bay has a wild beauty all of its own. Although the land is farmed it is extremely isolated and was once a favourite haunt of smugglers who landed their cargoes on the deserted beaches. The cliffs at White Nothe provided part of the setting for *Moonfleet*, J. M. Falkner's famous novel about the Dorset smugglers.

Another author, Llewelyn Powys, lived near White Nothe during the early part of this century. He loved the area so much that he expressed the wish to be buried here but initially his wishes were frustrated. He died abroad on 2 December 1939 at the age of fifty-five and, owing to the war which then raged in Europe, it was impossible to return his body to Dorset for burial. He was cremated in the country where he died and his ashes were eventually brought back to England when the war was over. They were buried to the right of the track which runs across the edge of Chaldon Down and their resting place is marked by a memorial stone carved by Elizabeth Muntz.

Take the A352 Wool to Dorchester road travelling towards Dorchester and having passed through East Knighton turn left by the Red Lion Inn following signs to Winfrith Newburgh. Bear left at the church on to the road to Lulworth Cove and Durdle Door.

After approximately two miles the road curves to the left at a place where it is crossed by some electricity cables supported by wooden posts. Two tracks, one to the left and one to the right, join the road at this point. This is Daggers Gate. Beside the beginning of the right-hand track is a rough lay-by which makes an excellent parking place for this walk.

Go through the gate on to the track beside which you have parked. The track forks almost immediately. Take the left-hand fork which leads up a slight slope, goes through a gate and then descends again towards a second gate.

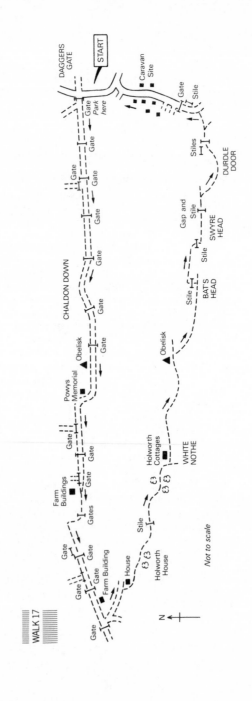

WALK 17

DAGGERS GATE

START

Caravan Site

Gate
Stile

Gate *Park here*

Gate
Gate

Gate
Gate

CHALDON DOWN

Gate
Gate

Gate
Gate

Gate

Obelisk
Powys Memorial

Gate

Gate
Farm Buildings

Gates
Gate

Gate

Farm Buildings

Gate
Gate
Farm Building

Gate
Gate
House

Gate
Gate

Holworth House

Stile

Holworth Cottages

WHITE NOTHE

Obelisk

BAT'S HEAD

Stile

Stile

SWYRE HEAD

Gap and Stile

Stiles

DURDLE DOOR

N

Not to scale

Just beyond this gate a second track leads through a gate on the right, but disregard this and go straight on, following the original track, which has now become grass covered, across first one field and then another.

In the third field the track curves round the top of a steep-sided hollow where there are good views of the sea, and then climbs a hill to a gate at the top. Beyond this it runs along the ridge going through another gate and passing an obelisk on the right-hand side.

Continue to follow the track as it swings inland beside the fence. The memorial to Llewelyn Powys is just ahead on the right. Beyond it the track curves left again and within a short distance is joined by a second track which comes through a gate on the right. This is marked 'No Right of Way' so ignore it and carry straight on, passing through another gate. At this point the view of the sea is hidden but there is a beautiful panorama of fields and hills to the right.

Not far beyond the gate another track leads away to the right by some farm buildings but once again this is marked 'No Right of Way' so continue straight ahead. The track degenerates into a path and leads to a pair of gates. Go through the smaller of these and bear slightly right to follow the fence. At the corner of the field swing left and continue to follow the fence down the slope. This will bring you to the bottom right-hand corner of the field where there is a gate on the right and another straight ahead. Go through the one straight ahead and follow the track on down the slope passing a track which leads through a gate to the right.

The track you are following goes through a gate and passes some farm buildings on the left to reach another gate. Just before it, turn left on to another track which forks almost immediately. Take the left-hand fork which heads towards a white house.

On reaching the house turn right and, keeping the garden fence on your left, walk down to the corner of it. At the corner bear left across the slope to the beginning of a narrow path at the upper edge of a patch of scrub. This is the beginning of the cliff path. It swings swiftly to the left and follows the edge of the cliff passing over a stile and winding through some scrub to Holworth cottages.

Follow the path to the seaward side of the cottages where it forks. The right-hand branch leads to the cliff edge so keep to the left which runs along beside the wall and then continues along the cliff edge. This will bring you to another obelisk, just beyond which the path forks. Take the right-hand branch which is the wider and leads obliquely down the hillside.

Continue along the path as it leads up the other side of the valley and up to the ridge beyond. Just over the crest of the ridge there is a stile in the fence on the left. Cross this and turn right to follow the fence down the hill. It is a steep descent and is better tackled on this side of the fence than the other. At the bottom cross back over a second stile to rejoin the cliff path.

Turn left and climb up to the next ridge. Once again the views are magnificent. The path passes through a gap in a fence with a stile beside it and then descends another steep slope. Here it is also advisable to leave the main path, this time to take a narrow one which runs beside the fence on the left.

At the bottom of the slope the main path forks. Take the right-hand branch which curves along the cliff edge. At the top of the slope there is a good view of Durdle Door straight ahead and this becomes even better as the path curves round to reach a place where there is a fence and a stile with a second stile in the fence to the left.

Ignore the left-hand stile and keep to the main path. Where it forks just beyond the stile keep to the left and follow it round to join a wide gravel track that climbs the hill. Near the top of the slope there is a stile on the right but disregard this and carry straight on passing through a gap beside the gate on the hilltop.

Follow the track straight ahead, ignoring two tracks which lead to the caravan site on the left. The track goes through a gap in the hedge marked 'Caution Ramps Speed Limit 5 mph' and becomes a metalled lane. It then leads through the main part of the caravan park and up to the road. At the road turn left and walk along the verge until you reach the car.

Walk 18   The Dorsetshire Gap

5½ miles (8·5 km)

OS sheet 194
Start: Melcombe Bingham

This walk is well off the beaten track and much of it involves walking across open fields on ill-defined paths. Yet, for those interested in the wild-life of the countryside it can be a very rewarding walk. This is an area where a wide variety of flowers are to be seen and timid creatures, such as foxes, hare and deer, abound.

The Dorsetshire Gap is a deep cut through the hills leading from Nettlecombe Tout to Higher Melcombe. It is a fascinating place being so completely hidden from all sides that the walker comes upon it with startling suddenness. It is part of one of the county's oldest trackways and in more recent times has also served as a convenient camping place for the local gypsies.

Higher Melcombe is a tiny hamlet which nestles in a valley amongst the hills. Its main feature is a curious old manor house, part of which was once a chapel.

Turn off the A354, Blandford to Puddletown road in Milborne St. Andrew and follow the signs to Cheselbourne. Pass through the village heading for Melcombe Bingham. On the outskirts of Melcombe Bingham village the road comes to a crossroad marked 'Cross Lanes'. At this point turn left into the entrance to the private road to Higher Melcombe and park by the houses on the left, being sure to keep well in to the left-hand side of the road.

Walk past the group of houses and on up the road to Higher Melcombe. As you enter the hamlet there are some farm buildings on the right and the old manor house is on the left. Beyond this the road goes down a slight slope, passing a duck pond on the right to terminate at a group of farm buildings and cottages near the head of the valley.

Take the track which goes to the right of the large metal barn with the weather vane on top. This track leads between another barn on the left and a tractor shed on the right to a farm gate. Go through this gate and obliquely left across the lane beyond.

There is a large barn directly opposite the gate you have just come through and beside it, to the left, a couple of metal gates. Go through the left-hand one of these and then walk straight ahead keeping the concrete wall on your right and passing another farm building on the left.

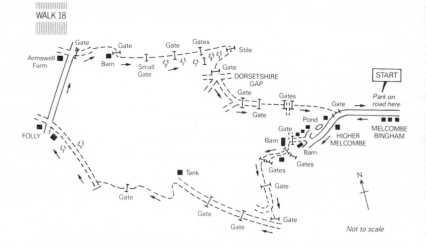

Having passed beyond the farm buildings the track broadens. There are two gateways on the left. Go through the second of these and turn left to follow the hedge up the hill. There is a gate in the hedge on the left but ignore this and leave the field by the gateway at the top. From here the track which had become distinct just before the gate, curves up the hill to the left. Follow it until it turns right at the top of the slope. Then leave it and go straight ahead.

There is a gate in the left-hand hedge but ignore this and go to the very top of the field. The fence bends round to form an extension; in the right-hand corner of this there is a second gate. Go through this and turn right to follow the track along the ridge. It leads through first one field gate and then another, after which it becomes rather indistinct but still carry on straight ahead towards a metal water tank on the horizon.

Just beyond the tank another rather indistinct track crosses the first. Turn left on to this and head towards a gap in the hedge. Do not go through this gap but turn right just before it to follow the edge of the field.

When you reach the corner of the field bear slightly left and then right to reach a gate beneath some trees. Beyond this gate is a narrow path which passes a small gate on the left and then heads down a slope to a track. Turn right and follow the track which leads down to the road.

Turn right and walk along the road until you come to Armswell Farm on the left. Directly opposite the farm entrance is a gate. Go through this and follow the track up the hill. At the top of the slope where the track becomes indistinct head towards the barn.

Turn right to go through the gate beside the barn and then sharp left keeping the hedge on the left. At the far side of the field go through the small gate and then carry on straight ahead skirting the wood on the right.

Where the wood curves away to the right go straight ahead. This will take you up a rather steep slope at the top of which is a gate in a hedge. Go through this and down the slope beyond still keeping the trees on the right. This will bring you to the far side of the field where there are two gates near a water trough. Go through the left one and carry on straight ahead passing a second stand of trees on the left.

Where there is a break in the belt of trees to the right there is a stile in the fence. Cross this and turn sharp right to walk beside the trees until you reach another gate. Beyond it there are four tracks. Take the second track on the left which slopes steeply downhill through the Dorsetshire Gap.

Near the bottom of the slope the track is joined by another from the right but disregard this and carry straight on passing through a metal gate into a narrow lane. This leads to another metal gate beyond which is a field.

Go straight ahead keeping the hedge on the right to reach a gate at the far side of the field. It gives access to the head of a lane. Cross this and go through the gate directly opposite and then carry straight on, still keeping the hedge on the right.

Part way along the hedge there is a gate to the right but ignore this and head for a second at the corner of the field. It opens on to the road. Turn left and walk back along the road to the car.

Walk 19   Puddletown Forest

4½ miles (7 km)

OS sheet 194
Start: Puddletown Forest car park

Puddletown Forest is a pleasant wooded area to the east of Dorchester. Parts of it are made up of deciduous trees but the majority is composed of conifers planted by the Forestry Commission.

Although the forest is so close to the county town and within easy reach of a major road it is a quiet place where a wide selection of plants and animals are to be seen. One of its main attractions in early summer are the rhododendrons which transform parts of the forest into a riot of brilliant colour. The best place to admire these is the Rhododendron Mile which is an avenue of rhododendron bushes lining the narrow road that runs through the forest from Puddletown. This avenue was planted by the Brymer family in the days before the land was leased to the Forestry Commission.

Take the A35 trunk road from Dorchester to Puddletown and, having passed the Prince of Wales public house on the left, turn right into Coombe Road. Follow this narrow road out of the town and up a hill lined with beech trees. From here it carries straight on for some distance and then swings sharply to the left. As the road turns left it is joined by a gravel lane to the right. This leads up a slight slope at the top of which there is a car park on the left.

Leave the car park by the gate at the far end. This is normally kept locked but there is a gap beside it.

Having passed the gate follow the track straight ahead. It winds its way through the woods first climbing a slight slope then dipping down the far side before climbing once more.

As the track flattens out at the top of the second rise it curves to the left and a narrow path leads up a slope through the trees. Ignore this path and carry on along the track. Not far from here it becomes grass covered and is joined by a second path from the left. Still keep to the track. It heads towards a stand of fir trees and is joined by a minor grassy track from the right.

Keep to the main track which swings left through the trees and within a very short distance comes to a place where four tracks meet. Turn right at this point.

Not far along the track it is joined by three more, two from the left and one from the right. Ignore all these and carry on to where the

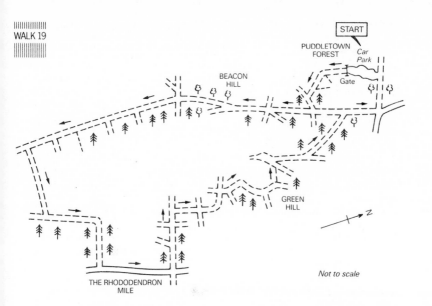

START

PUDDLETOWN
FOREST   Car
          Park

Gate

BEACON
HILL

GREEN
HILL

N

THE RHODODENDRON
MILE

Not to scale

main track forks then keep to the right. Unlike its counterpart, this branch is not grass covered. It leads on through the trees and eventually emerges at a place where five tracks meet. Take the one straight ahead.

This track runs along beside a stand of fir trees on the left whilst on the right it is bordered by bushes and low lying scrub. After some distance a track leads away through the trees to the left. Disregard this and go straight on. This will take you past a deep hollow on the left with another grassy track beside it.

Still keep straight on and soon the track will bring you to the top of a steep slope from which there is a pleasant view across the valley. At this point a narrow path leads downhill to the left between some rhododendron bushes. Take no notice of this and follow the track down the slope. The descent is steep but fairly short and at the bottom the track is joined by another which loops round from the left. Ignore this and follow the track straight ahead. It goes down a second less precipitous slope and then swings to a point where a narrower secondary track leads straight ahead.

Keep to the main track which curves to the left and heads towards some trees. Near the trees it is joined by another minor track as it swings left again. Ignore this and keep to the main track which soon turns right and leads down to the road.

Turn left to follow the road. This is part of the Rhododendron Mile and at the right time of the year the bushes on either side are ablaze with colour.

The road goes over a slight rise and is joined by a track from the left.

Take this track which is the beginning of a forest walk. It leads straight ahead through the trees and is then joined by another track from the left. Disregard this and go straight on following the second forest walk sign.

As the track emerges from the trees it is crossed by a second track. Still carry straight on and within about fifty yards you will come to a track on the right. Follow this up the hill towards a stand of fir trees. About two-thirds of the way up it is crossed by another track, the left-hand part of which is rather indistinct. Ignore this and go on up the slope towards the trees.

The track curves left and is crossed by another. Turn right on to this and, ignoring the track which leads away to the right, follow the branch that curves left by the trees. This soon swings to the right and goes down a slope. At the bottom of the slope a track marked 'Forest walk 8' leads away to the right. Disregard this and follow the original track. It curves left again and then goes through a wood.

Just before the track enters the trees it is joined by a narrow path which comes down a hill to the left. Turn on to this and follow it up the hill and turn left on to the track at the top.

Within a very short distance the track widens and a narrow track curves sharply away to the right through the trees. Turn on to this and when you come to a place where it forks keep to the left-hand branch. This goes straight ahead down a slope.

At the bottom of the slope it meets another track in a T-junction. Turn right and follow this track back to the road. The track which leads up to the car park is now on your left.

Walk 20

Osmington Mills

3 miles (4·5 km)

OS sheet 194
Start: Upton

Osmington Mills is one of the prettiest places on the Dorset coast. Separated from the village of Osmington by the main Weymouth road, this tiny hamlet lies in a pleasant valley through which a small stream makes its way to the sea. Osmington Mills is where John Constable came to paint his famous *Weymouth Bay*, and even today the view is almost unspoilt.

Ringstead Bay, overlooked to the east by the great cliff of White Nothe, is a delightful place. One of its main claims to fame is the mystery of the old village. It became completely deserted during the fifteenth century and all that remains of it today are a few grassy humps in a field. Why the village was deserted is completely unknown but there are two theories put forward to explain it. One is that the village was destroyed during a French raid in 1420 when the villagers took refuge in the church which the raiders burnt. The other is that the population was wiped out by the Black Death.

Take the A352 from Dorchester travelling towards Wareham. Having passed through Broadmayne the road leads to a roundabout just outside the village of Warmwell. Turn right here on to the A353 which is signposted Weymouth. This will take you through Poxwell. Just beyond the village, after the road swings right, turn left on to a narrow road marked 'Ringstead 1½'. Go through Upton and park on the left-hand verge just beyond the sign on the right which marks the end of the hamlet.

Carry on along the road. As it bends to the left there is a sign to Ringstead on the right. Beside this sign a metalled track marked 'Footpath only' leads away to the right. Turn on to this and follow it up the slope to where it forks. Take the left-hand fork which goes through a gate and is labelled 'footpath'.

Where the track forks again keep to the right. After passing a chalet on the right the track leads to a gate with a stile beside it. Cross the stile and carry straight on ignoring a second stile in the fence to the left. The track narrows to a path and leads down to the road.

Turn left and then almost immediately right on to another footpath which goes down a slope through some trees passing some caravans on the left. At the bottom of the slope the path is blocked by another stile. Beyond this it curves slightly to the left and then leads across the field skirting a white house on the right.

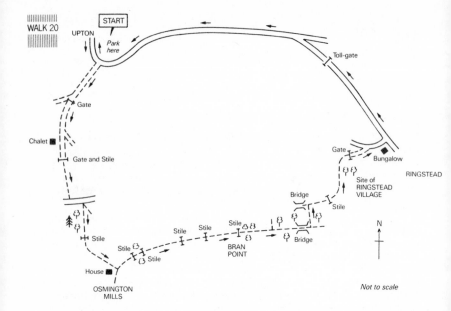

At the corner of the white house's garden the path crosses a ditch and then joins another faint grassy path at right-angles. To continue the walk you must turn left here and follow the path up the slope to the cliff top but, before doing this, explore the path to the right. It leads down to the delightful little hamlet of Osmington Mills and a very short walk will take you past the pretty thatched cottages to the rocky shoreline from which there are beautiful views.

Having followed the left-hand path up the slope you will come to two stiles set one in front of the other amongst some bushes near the cliff top. Cross both of these and continue to follow the path keeping the cliff on your right.

After some distance the path leads down a slope to a stile. Cross this and continue along the path which crosses another stile and carries on down the hill. This will bring you to a place where there is a stile to the left and another straight ahead. Ignore the one to the left and having crossed the other, follow the path through the bushes. Beyond them the path runs beside a fence at the end of which another path leads away to the left. Disregard this and carry straight on following the path down the slope through the trees.

Cross the bridge at the bottom and turn left on to a path which borders the stream. Within a very short distance the path is crossed by another which comes over the stream from the left. Turn right and walk up the slope to a stile at the edge of the wood. Cross the stile and turn obliquely left to walk across the field towards a group of sycamore trees. This will lead you through the humps and hollows which mark the site of the old Ringstead village.

Pass to the left of the sycamore trees and then bear right to reach the field gate. Go through this and follow the track up to the lane then turn right. The lane goes through a gateway passing a bungalow on the right and leads up to the road.

Turn left and follow the road up the hill. It passes the toll-gate on the summit and then dips down to join another road in a T-junction. Turn left and walk down this road until you reach the place where you parked the car.

Walk 21   The Heart of the Hardy Country

4 miles (6 km)

OS sheet 194
Start : Higher Bockhampton

For all who know and love the works of Thomas Hardy the area around Higher and Lower Bockhampton will be of special interest. This is the true heart of the Hardy country, the place where he was born, grew to maturity and wrote two of his most famous novels.

The delightful little church at Stinsford is where he worshipped as a boy. It has a window dedicated to his memory and under one of the churchyard trees his heart lies buried beside the remains of other members of his family.

Stinsford is the village of Mellstock immortalised in his novel *Under the Greenwood Tree* and in this work the church and its choir are vividly portrayed. The gallery which they used has since been demolished but the little church still retains much of the atmosphere that it must have had when Hardy knew it.

Lower Bockhampton with its little humpbacked bridge and picturesque thatched cottages was also a village which Hardy knew well. It was here, at the age of eight, that he began his scholastic career. He spent one year at the village school in Lower Bockhampton before entering a Nonconformist school in Dorchester.

Hardy's cottage which stands in the hamlet of Higher Bockhampton at the edge of Puddletown Forest is a beautiful little thatched cottage. Thomas Hardy was born here on 2 June 1840 and in it he wrote *Under the Greenwood Tree* and *Far From The Madding Crowd*. Beside the cottage stands a simple stone monument erected by some of the author's American admirers. Today the cottage is the property of the National Trust. Its exterior may be viewed from the garden from 11 a.m. to 6 p.m. during the months of March to October and the interior can be seen by appointment with the tenant.

Take the turning off the A35 Dorchester to Bournemouth road marked 'Higher Bockhampton ¾, Lower Bockhampton 1¼'. This is on the right-hand side coming from Dorchester and about midway between the centre of Dorchester and Puddletown. The road initially leads up the side of a hill. Just over the brow is a lane on the left marked 'Higher Bockhampton and Hardy's Cottage'. Turn left and follow this lane for about a hundred yards before turning right on to a gravel track which leads to a free car park.

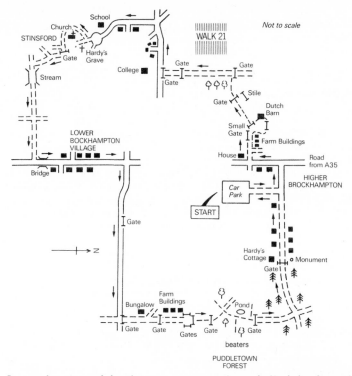

WALK 21

Not to scale

School
Church
STINSFORD
Hardy's Grave
Gate
Stream
College
Gate
Gate
Gate
Gate
Gate
Stile
Dutch Barn
Small Gate
Farm Buildings
House
Road from A35
HIGHER BROCKHAMPTON
LOWER BOCKHAMPTON VILLAGE
Bridge
Car Park
START
Gate
N
Hardy's Cottage
Monument
Gate
Bungalow
Farm Buildings
Pond
Gate
Gate
Gates
Gate
Gate

beaters

PUDDLETOWN FOREST

Leave the car park by the way you came in and climb back up the lane to the road. Turn left passing two white bungalows on the left.

After about a hundred yards a gravel farm track crosses the road. Turn right and follow the track passing a house on the left and some farm buildings on the right.

The track eventually curves to the right and ends at a Dutch barn. As it does so a small metal gate gives access to a field straight ahead. Go through this gate and follow the fence on the right down the hill to a second gate. There is a stile beside it to the right but ignore this and go through the gate and bear right to follow the edge of this field to where it slopes down and joins a track in the valley. Turn left on to the track.

Follow the track through two field gates to the road. Turn right and walk along the road. It leads up a hill. Across a field to the left a large white mansion house is to be seen: this is the Dorset College of Agriculture, Kingston Maurward.

At the top of the hill the road passes a group of four white houses on the left and then dips downhill again to pass the entrance to the college drive. Not far beyond this is a turning on the left marked 'Stinsford Church, Stinsford School'. Take this turning; it will lead you past some of the college's farm buildings on the left before curving

71

left and then right, skirting Stinsford School and finishing at the church.

Enter the churchyard through the small gateway. A tarmac path leads straight ahead for a short distance and then forks, the left fork leading down to the corner of the church and the right curving round behind it to end at a similar gateway in the far corner of the churchyard. The right-hand path is the one to take for it leads past the church door and enables the walker to pause for a few moments to study the interior of the church which Hardy knew so well.

Before doing this, however, take a short diversion on to the left-hand path. Beside it, to the left, are the graves of the Hardy family. Here lie buried the author's parents and his wife. She is buried together with her husband's heart. The remainder of his ashes lie in Poets Corner, Westminster Abbey.

Having followed the right-hand path round behind the church, leave the churchyard by the small wooden gateway. Turn right and follow the gravel track which passes an extension to the graveyard on the right and then a few more graves beyond the metal fence on the left. Where the graveyard on the right ends at a small metal gate the path forks. Take the left-hand fork which runs along beside the metal fence and then turns sharp left where another narrower path joins it from the right. Turn left to follow the main path.

After some distance a farm track crosses the path at right-angles. Ignore this and carry straight on to where the path ends at the bridge. Turn left across the bridge and follow the road through Lower Bockhampton village to the crossroads. Turn right on to the road which leads up a slight hill.

At the top of the hill turn left on to a gravel track marked Pine Lodge Farm. Follow the track through two gates passing some farm buildings on the left. Where the track ends at three field entrances carry straight on keeping the hedge on your left. This will bring you to a gate in the far corner of the field. Go through the gate and follow the path for a short distance to where three paths and a track join. Turn sharp right and then left passing some fire beaters on your right and ignoring a narrow path which leads down a slope by an oak tree marked with the figure 15. Go straight on following the path up a hill through some trees.

At the top of the slope a second narrow path skirts a pond to the left and there is a gate across the track. Disregard the path and go through the opening beside the gate on to the track which leads straight ahead. It is signposted 'Hardy's Cottage'.

Follow this track until it passes through a group of trees and crosses another track at right-angles. Turn left and follow this track through the woods to the gate. Go through the gap beside the gate on to the gravel lane. The stone monument erected to Thomas Hardy is to your right and the thatched cottage to the left is Hardy's cottage. Carry on along the gravel lane until it joins the metalled lane which leads up to the road. Turn left and follow the gravel track back to the car.

Walk 22   White Horse Hill

3 miles (4·5 km)

OS sheet 194
Start: Sutton Poyntz

Lying on the outskirts of Weymouth the northern part of Sutton Poyntz is a haven of peaceful undeveloped beauty. Here are to be seen old thatched barns, stone cottages and a pond bordered with willow trees where a variety of ducks swim on the clear water.

Osmington is another grey stone village set back from the main road. John Constable spent his honeymoon here. He was so impressed with the village that he painted it. *Osmington Village* is one of his lesser known works but it was also during his stay here that he painted the more famous *Weymouth Bay*.

White Horse Hill gets its name from the large figure of a man on a horse which has been carved into the chalk of its south slope. It is a huge figure, 280 ft long and 320 ft high but, unlike many hill carvings, it is not very old. It was first cut out in 1808 under the direction of a local bookseller and is a portrait of King George III on his horse. The work was done to commemorate this king's association with Weymouth. Together with his brother, the Duke of Gloucester, King George paid regular visits to the town as a result of which it grew into a fashionable and wealthy seaside resort.

From Weymouth sea front follow the signs 'A352 Wareham and Wimborne'. On the far side of Preston turn left opposite the Ship Inn into Sutton Road. This is signposted 'Sutton Poyntz'. Follow the road to where it divides and take the right-hand fork which is labelled Sutton Poyntz and Springhead. Drive up this road until you come to a public house on the right called The Springhead. Park opposite it on the left beside the duck pond.

Walk straight on to where the road ends and turn right on to a track marked 'No Through Road. Footpath to White Horse & Hunt Bros.' Pass the joiner's yard on your left and carry straight on to reach a gate labelled 'Footpath only. No horses'. Go through this and then straight ahead through a second gate which opens on to a field.

Walk straight across the field to a gate at the far side and then continue across the next field to another gate. Beyond this a path leads away to the left. Ignore it and carry straight on following the hedge on the right. This will bring you to a small gate in the bottom right-hand corner of the field. Go through it and straight ahead once more to

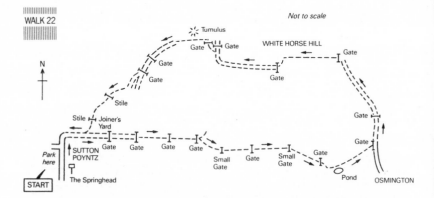

reach a gate at the far side of the next field. From this field there are good views of the White Horse on the hill to the left.

Cross yet another field going over a double stile in the hedge on the far side and then bear slightly right to reach a gate in the bottom right-hand corner of the field beyond. Go through it and bear right to follow the fence that borders the pond.

Leave the fence where it turns right and carry straight on along the narrow path that heads towards the houses. This will bring you to a gate in the corner of the field which opens on to the end of a lane.

Turn left to follow a track marked 'Bridleway to White Horse Hill'. It leads between hedges to a gate and then bears left up the hillside.

At the top of the hill turn left to pass through a gate on to a path which leads straight ahead following the fence on the right. The field it is skirting lies right on the ridge of the hill and there are good views of Weymouth Bay and Portland to the left.

At the far side of the field the path curves round to a gate. Go through it and follow the track straight ahead. After some distance it swings to the right and ends at a gate. Leave the track to go to the left of the gate. This will bring you to a second gate in the field fence. Go through it and turn sharp left to pass between a tumulus and the fence. This will lead you to a track which goes down the hill. It passes through a gate and on down the hillside from which there are yet more good views of Weymouth and Portland.

About half way down the hill the track leads through another gate and divides. Take the right-hand branch; it runs along the ridge of the gully through which the left-hand branch passes.

Near the end of the ridge turn right and go down the slope to a stile in the hedge. Cross the stile and follow the narrow path that runs obliquely across the field to a second stile beyond which is the joiner's yard. Go through the yard and turn right to follow the track back to where you left the car.

Walk 23   Portland

4 miles (6 km)

OS sheet 194
Start: Suckthumb Quarry

The Isle of Portland is not a proper island but a peninsula which is joined to the mainland by the long strip of shingle known as the Chesil Beach. It is unlike any other part of Dorset and has a character all of its own. Virtually no trees grow on its high plateau and the surface of the land is pitted with the quarries from which the famous Portland stone is extracted.

Portland Bill is the southern tip of the peninsula. It has an impressive rugged coastline where layers of limestone rock shelve down to the sea. There are caves here and two lighthouses. The younger is still in use and is often open to the public.

The old lighthouse was once the home of Marie Stopes, the pioneer of birth control. Today it is a bird observatory and field centre.

Towards the northern end of Portland is an old prison which is now used as a borstal training centre. During the Victorian era convicts from this prison built the great breakwater that encloses Portland harbour. This is one of the largest and safest naval bases in the world and a great variety of naval craft are to be seen in the waters around Portland.

From Weymouth follow the road signs for Portland. This will take you along the road which leads over the Chesil Beach. At the far end of the beach start following the road signs to Portland Bill. They will lead you through Fortuneswell and Easton, and beyond this the Pennsylvania Castle Hotel is on the left-hand side. Having passed the Pennsylvania Castle Hotel on the left followed by a road marked 'Weston ½' on the right, the road curves right to pass Suckthumb Quarry on the right. Just before it there is ample parking space on the top of a hillock to the left.

Leave the parking area and walk on down the road passing the quarry on the right. This will lead you past a single house set back from the road on the left. Just beyond it turn left on to a track marked 'Public Footpath'.

Where the track forks keep to the left-hand branch which continues along the cliff, ignoring a quarry entrance on the right. Not far beyond this the track forks again. Still keep to the left so that you are following the edge of the cliff. This will bring you to a group of fishermen's huts and winches.

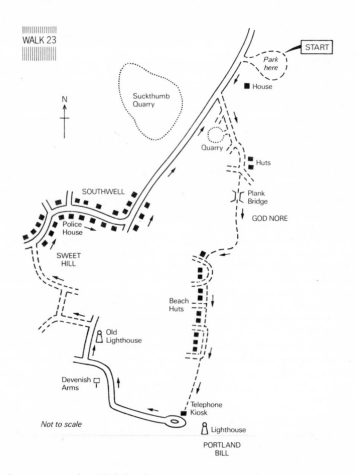

START

Park here

■ House

Suckthumb Quarry

N

Quarry

■ Huts

SOUTHWELL

Plank Bridge

GOD NORE

Police House

SWEET HILL

Beach Huts

Old Lighthouse

Devenish Arms

Not to scale

Telephone Kiosk

■ Lighthouse

PORTLAND BILL

Ignore a track which leads to the right and another which follows the cliff to the left. Go straight ahead taking a path which climbs a slight slope and is partially blocked by a rectangular lump of stone.

The path skirts some fields to the right and crosses a drainage ditch by a narrow plank bridge before leading straight ahead towards the Bill. This will take you past another winch beneath which there is a large and very impressive cave. Beyond this the path goes through a group of beach huts to join a track which comes down from the road to the right.

Follow the track straight ahead then leave it where it swings right beside a yellow sign and carry on towards the red and white lighthouse. Ignore a second track to the right and carry straight on. This will bring you to where the faint grassy path joins a gravel track. Follow this straight ahead. Where it turns abruptly right beside a black notice-board leave it and go straight on passing between the stone blocks and across the common land towards the telephone kiosk.

This telephone kiosk stands beside the turning circle where the road ends at Portland Bill and it is a good idea to abandon the walk for a short time at this point to explore the Bill itself. Beyond the lighthouse, which is often open to visitors, are impressive cliffs where shelves of rock provide convenient seats on which to sit and admire the view. Pulpit Rock is to the right and marks the very southern-most tip of Portland. It is a tall rectangular block of limestone against which rests a slab provided with footholds.

Continue the walk by going back to the turning circle and walking up the road passing the car park on your left. The road swings left by the Devenish Arms and then right to pass the old lighthouse on the right. Just beyond the lighthouse turn left on to a track marked 'Public Footpath'.

Where the track forks at the top of the hill take the right-hand branch. It leads along the hilltop giving a good view of the prison in the distance and then swings left. At this point it is joined by a grassy track from the right, but ignore this and continue along the main track which is now bordered by stone walls.

When the track emerges on to the road turn right. Follow the road round to the right and at the junction take the right-hand fork, passing a police house on your right. You are now in Southwell Street.

At the next junction follow the road round to the left. It is signposted 'Easton 1½ Weymouth 8'. This will bring you back past the quarry on your left to where you left the car.

Walk 24   Maiden Castle

3 miles (4·5 km)

OS sheet 194
Start: Maiden Castle car park

Situated high on a hill one mile south of the county town of Dorchester, Maiden Castle is one of the largest and most formidable hill-forts in England. It was built over 2,000 years ago and incorporated a smaller early Iron Age village which was protected by a single rampart and ditch.

The present hill-fort is nearly half a mile long and a quarter of a mile wide. It is oval in shape and bordered by three, and in many places four, lines of ramparts which are between 60 ft and 90 ft in height. The circumference of the outer rampart is almost two miles and at either end are entrances guarded by complicated series of earthworks. Maiden Castle was still a thriving town when the Romans came to Britain and one of the bloodiest battles of the Roman conquest was fought beneath its walls. This took place in AD 43 or 44. The Roman army under the leadership of Vespasian met strong resistance from the townspeople and, having won their way into the castle, retaliated with unwarranted ferocity killing large numbers of men, women and children.

Not long after this the surviving remnants of the population left the ruins of the hilltop town. They moved to the new Roman settlement of Durnovaria which was on the site of the modern town of Dorchester in the valley below.

For almost four centuries Maiden Castle lay deserted and forgotten and then, in about AD 380, a small group returned to build a temple there. Part of the old fortress became the temple precinct and a tiny two-roomed house was erected to accommodate the priest.

Take the A354 from Dorchester travelling towards Weymouth and turn right on to the road signposted to Maiden Castle. Follow the road to the end and park in the car park at the foot of Maiden Castle.

Go through the small gate which gives access to the monument from the car park and take the track on the right. This leads up the hill beside the fence and will bring you to a gate. Go through it and continue along the track which descends the slope and passes through another gate. Beyond this second gate follow the grassy path which leads straight ahead between low hills and eventually meets a gate that opens on to the lane.

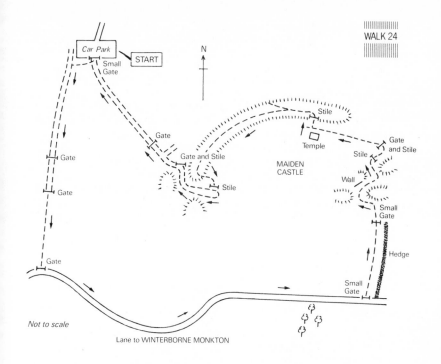

Car Park

START

Small
Gate

N

Gate

Gate

Gate and Stile

Gate

Stile

Gate

Stile

Stile

MAIDEN
CASTLE

Temple

Stile

Gate
and Stile

Wall

Small
Gate

Hedge

Small
Gate

Small
Gate

Not to scale

Lane to WINTERBORNE MONKTON

Turn left and walk along the lane. It will lead you past Maiden Castle, which is on the hilltop to your left, and gives a very good impression of the size of the monument.

After about half a mile the lane is approached by a belt of trees from the right. Approximately a quarter of a mile beyond this the fence on the left is interrupted by a hedge which comes down the hill from the earthwork. Just before this hedge reaches the lane there is a small gate in the fence. Go through this and follow the footpath up the hill beside the hedge to reach another small gate at the top. Having passed through this gate take the grassy path straight ahead which leads up on to the ramparts.

At the top of the first rise swing slightly left to follow the path through a gap in the next ridge and then curve to the right passing a stone wall on the left. Beyond this the path turns left again to pass through another rampart. On the far side turn sharp right to cross a stile in the fence and then immediately left over a second stile beside a gate. This gives access to the open area at the top of the castle.

Follow the footpath straight ahead; it will bring you to an enclosure on the left containing the remains of the Roman temple and the priest's house. There is a small gateway which enables visitors to go into the temple enclosure and it is well worth pausing for a few moments to study the ruins.

Leave the path beside the entrance to the temple compound and turn right to cross a stile on to the ramparts. From here there is a magnificent view across the valley to the county town of Dorchester.

Turn left to follow the ridge of the inner rampart. After a short distance a path goes down into the ditch to the right but ignore this and carry straight on.

The ridge eventually ends beside the castle's main entrance and gives a good view of the complex series of ramparts which guarded this important point. Turn left to descend the ridge and then sharp right over a stile on to the track which led into the castle. Turn right and walk down the track following the fence round to the right and then to the left.

Ignore a stile by a gate on the right and carry on down the track. It curves to the right once more and then divides to head towards two gates. Go through the left-hand one and then walk on down the slope to the car park.

Walk 25   Sherborne Deer Park

3 miles (4·5 km)

OS sheet 183
Start: Goathill

This can be rather a wet walk, parts of it being across low-lying meadows and other parts along narrow footpaths through tall undergrowth. Waterproof footwear and clothing are strongly recommended for all but the longest spells of dry weather. Yet, in spite of its drawbacks, this can be a very pleasant and interesting walk.

For those who want a real taste of country life this walk is superb. Parts of it lead through the grounds of Sherborne Castle. This was built by Sir Walter Raleigh but later became the property of the Digby family. Its park was laid out by 'Capability' Brown and does great credit to his genius.

Pinford is one of the farms on the estate. It is surrounded by fields in which flocks of geese are to be seen.

From here the route leads through the park where herds of deer graze beneath the trees. They often pause at what they consider a reasonable distance to watch the passer-by, rather than diving for cover at the first signs of approach, and so the chance of getting good views of them is very high. Then the path leads past the keeper's cottage where there are pens for young pheasants.

Take the A30 out of Sherborne heading towards Shaftesbury and just on the outskirts of Milborne Port turn right on to a road signposted to Goathill. Where this road forks take the left-hand branch which is marked 'Stourton Caundle'. Drive up the hill and park in the lay-by on the left under the trees.

Walk back down the road and at the junction bear to the right following the sign to Goathill. Carry on until you come to the church on the left. Turn left beside it on to a track marked 'Pinford 1'.

Go straight ahead, passing some cottages on the left and some farm buildings on the right, to leave the farmyard by a gate at the far side. Follow the track past the duck pond on your left. The track then bears slightly right and is crossed by another which comes down a slope to the right. Ignore this and go straight ahead through the gate.

Leave the track and bear left to follow the fence until you come to a gate which leads into the wood on the left. At this point turn right and cross the field to another gate on the far side. Go through it and turn left. This brings you almost immediately to two gates one in front of

81

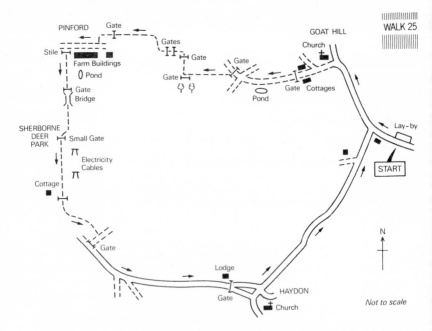

the other. Pass through both of these and turn right to follow the fence along two sides of the field to a gate near the farm buildings.

Leave the field by this gate and turn left on to the track which swings right to pass the farm buildings on the left. Just beyond them turn left over a stile and cross the field, passing the farmhouse and the duck pond on your left. This will bring you to a small gate in the far corner of the field. It opens on to a bridge. Having crossed this keep straight on along the side of the next field to a second small gate in the wall at the top. Beyond this is the deer park.

A set of electricity cables supported on wooden poles crosses the park at this point. From the gate go straight ahead, keeping these cables on the left as you ascend the slope by a narrow and rather indistinct path through the undergrowth.

At the top of the slope there is a gamekeeper's cottage and some game pens. Go straight ahead through the narrow gate and follow the fence, passing the game pens on the left. At the end of the fence turn right and follow the track to where it meets a metalled drive in a T-junction. Turn left and follow the drive round to the left, ignoring two tracks which join it from the right.

The drive leads down through the park gates to join the road. Turn left and follow the road until you come to a junction on the right marked Stourton Caundle. Turn right here and walk back up the hill to where you left the car.

Walk 26   Cerne Abbas and Up Cerne

8 miles (12·5 km)

OS sheet 194
Start: Cerne Abbas

Cerne Abbas was once a thriving market and manufacturing town, but its industry died during the last century when it was by-passed by the railway. Today all that remains is a beautiful village which must be one of the most interesting in Dorset.

As its name suggests, Cerne Abbas once had a large abbey. It was a Benedictine foundation and was originally built in about AD 987 by Ethelmaer, Earl of Cornwall. During the eleventh century it was rebuilt on a lavish scale and became one of the richest abbeys in Dorset owning land as far away as Brownsea Island in Poole Harbour. It was also an important monastic school.

All this came to an end in 1539 when King Henry VIII had the abbey dissolved. Within forty years it was in ruins and today little remains except some humps in Beavoir meadow and the beautiful porch to the abbot's hall which stands in the grounds of the manor house. This house is owned by the Digby family and was used, together with the arched gateway to the graveyard, as part of the setting for the film *Tom Jones*.

In the far corner of the graveyard is St Augustine's Well. It is a wishing well and is said to have been struck by St Augustine with the words 'Cerno Deum'.

Further down the street from the manor house stands the ancient church with its interesting corbels, and directly opposite it is a fine terrace of late medieval houses.

By far the most interesting thing to be seen in Cerne Abbas must surely be the Cerne Abbas Giant. This is the large figure of a man carved into the side of the hill just north of the village. It is very old and was probably intended to represent an early British fertility god.

Up Cerne is a charming little hamlet with a beautiful manor house which dates from about 1600.

Take the A352 Sherborne road from Dorchester. When the road enters Cerne Abbas carry straight on until you reach the decontrol signs at the far end of Acreman Street. Just beyond the decontrol signs turn right and then sharp left to park in the lay-by. The Cerne Abbas Giant is on the hill to your right.

Follow the road down the hill keeping the Cerne Abbas Giant on

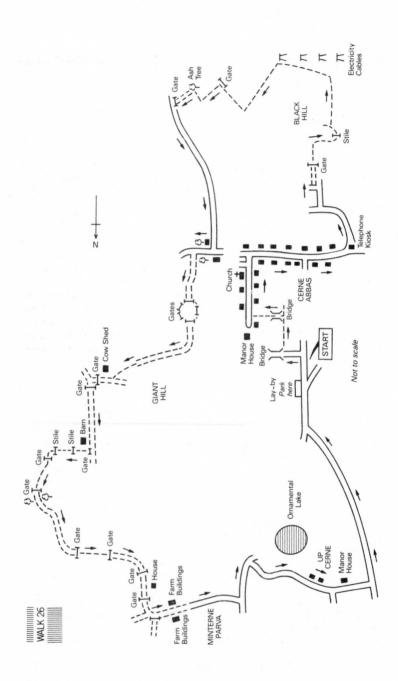

WALK 26

N

Gate
Ash Tree
Gate

BLACK HILL
Stile

Electricity Cables

Gate

Gate
Gates

Church

Telephone Kiosk

CERNE ABBAS

Bridge

Cow Shed
Gate

Manor House

Bridge

GIANT HILL

Gate
Barn
Stile
Stile
Gate

START

Gate
Gate
Gate

Lay-by
Park here

Gate
Gate
House

Farm Buildings

Not to scale

Ornamental Lake

UP CERNE

Manor House

Farm Buildings

MINTERNE PARVA

your left and then turn left into a narrow lane which has a grassy mound in the centre at the point where it joins the road. Just before the bridge turn right on to a path beside the stream.

Within a short distance the path forks. Take the left-hand branch which goes across a bridge and leads to a road.

Before turning right to follow the road down past the church it is well worth exploring the area to the left, for it is here that some of the village's most interesting features are to be found. In this direction the road comes to an end in front of the manor house. There is a drive to the right of the house which leads to the gardens at the back. Here you will find the porch of the abbot's hall. Although the gardens are private, the public are allowed access to this impressive ruin on payment of a small entrance fee in aid of a naval charity.

Beside the point where the drive emerges on to the road an arched gateway gives access to the graveyard. Go through this and follow the path straight ahead keeping the wall on your right and you will come to a short slope that goes down to St Augustine's Well.

The other path through the graveyard leads to Beavoir meadow where a series of humps and ridges mark the positions of the old abbey buildings.

To continue the walk go down the road past the church and turn right. Walk along the road until you come to a turning on the left by a telephone kiosk. This is Back Lane. Follow it round to the left and then turn right on to a road called Chescombe.

Within about fifty yards there is a turning to the left called Chescombe Close and beside the road sign a track leads straight ahead to a field gate. Take this track and then walk along the footpath which curves round the perimeter of the field to a stile in the top right-hand corner.

Cross the stile and turn left to follow the right-hand of the two paths for a short distance up the slope. Once clear of the bushes turn right on to one of the many narrow paths which run along the hillside.

Keep on along the hillside until it swings to the left to form the northern slope of a short valley. A line of wooden posts carrying electricity cables runs up the valley to the top of the hill at its head. Follow these and when you reach the one at the top of the slope turn left to follow the fence.

At the corner of the fence turn right and continue along it until you come to a gate. Turn left beside it on to a narrow path which runs across the hillside. This will bring you to the end of a wire fence. Turn right towards a small ash tree by the hedge and then left on to a track which runs down through a cattle pen to the road.

Turn left and follow the road down the hill to where it ends in a T-junction and then turn right. Just beyond the decontrol signs the road runs through a belt of trees and then curves to the left. At this point there is a lay-by on the right and a gravel track on the left. Turn on to this track and follow it to where a gate gives access to an open space, with two gates on the right, one on the left and another straight ahead. Go through the one straight ahead and follow the grassy track beyond.

The track curves to the right by a white notice-board and runs along the foot of the hill for some distance before climbing the slope. Near the top it degenerates into a path and becomes indistinct but carry straight on keeping the gully on your left. This will bring you to a place where the path joins a track. Turn right and pass behind the cow shed to reach a gate. Go through it and then sharp left through a second gate beyond which is a track. Walk along this until you reach a barn on the right. Just beyond it is a gate. Turn right through this gate and walk past the barn to cross a stile in the fence straight ahead.

Follow the hedge on the left to a second stile in the opposite corner of the field and beyond it turn left to go through a gate. Head slightly right down the hill to a gate at the far side of the field and then follow the rather indistinct track on down the slope. This will bring you to another gate which opens on to a field.

Cross the field to the gate at the far side and then walk on along the track. It leads through two more gates and then, having passed a house on the left, curves left at a point where it is joined by two other tracks from the right. Follow the track round to the left; it passes some farm buildings and then widens into a metalled lane which leads up to the road.

At the road turn left and walk round the bend to where a lane to Up Cerne leads away to the right. Turn on to this and follow it down the hill passing the ornamental lake on the left.

Having passed some cottages on the left the road forks. Take the left-hand branch which leads straight ahead with the manor house behind the hedge to the left.

This will bring you to a T-junction. Turn left and follow the lane to where it joins the road, then turn right. Follow the road back to where you left the car.

Walk 27   Fleet

3½ miles (5·5 km)

OS sheet 194
Start: Fleet

To anybody who has read John Meade Falkner's famous novel *Moonfleet* the tiny hamlet of East Fleet needs no introduction. Yet little remains of the original village in which the story was set. On 23 November 1824 there was a terrific storm. It blew a 90 ton sloop, the *Ebenezer*, on to the crest of the Chesil Beach and caused a mighty tidal wave which crashed through the village destroying the cottages and demolishing all but the chancel of the fine old church. A new church was built between the years 1827 and 1829 at the expense of the vicar, George Gould, and for some time the old building remained a neglected ruin. It has now been restored, although it is little more than a chapel and is not used for services. Beneath it the Mohun family vault is still in existence together with the old smugglers' secret passage which connects it with the Fleet.

The Fleet is a narrow salt-water lake that separates the mainland from the Chesil Beach. It is a shallow stretch of tidal water containing a great amount of seaweed and is not good for swimming. It does, however, support large numbers of fish such as bass, mullet and eels which are exploited by the local fishermen.

The Chesil Beach is a barrier of stones which connects the Isle of Portland with the mainland. It is over 17 miles in length and the size of the stones increases as it goes east. At the western end it is composed of a fine shingle whilst in the east some of the stones are as big as saucers.

The Chesil Beach has been the graveyard of many a fine sailing ship. Some, such as the *Ebenezer*, were lost in storms but others were lured to their deaths by wreckers who made a handsome livelihood from plundering vessels deliberately smashed on the Chesil stones.

Take the B3157 from Weymouth and turn left in Chickerell on to a road marked 'Fleet ½'. Drive down the road for approximately a mile. Having passed the church and two dwellings on the right the road curves slightly left. Just beyond this there are several parking places available under the trees on the right.

Walk on up the road. Where it divides three ways keep to the central branch which is marked 'Footpath Coastal Path ¾'. This leads through a gateway with a lodge on either side and on down a hill from which there is a view of the sea straight ahead.

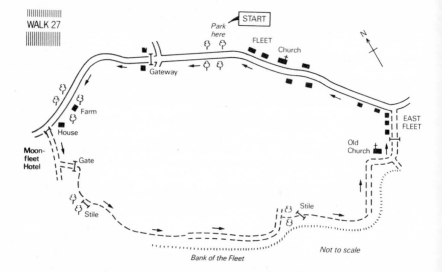

Near the bottom of the hill the road runs through a wood which screens some farm buildings on the left-hand side and then passes a red brick house on the left. Just beyond this, as the road swings right towards the Moonfleet Hotel, a track leads through a metal field gate to the left.

Follow the track through the gateway and on across the field to where it forks. Take the left-hand branch which leads through another gateway. Just beyond it turn sharp right on to a narrow path that skirts the field.

Continue on along this, ignoring a stile which leads into the wood on the right, until you come to the far corner of the field. From here take the path that leads straight ahead between the fence on the left and the waters of the Fleet on the right.

After about a quarter of a mile the fence comes to an end. Carry straight on following the wide grassy track which borders the Fleet. This will bring you to a place where the expanse of water widens. The track bears left to continue along the bank for a short distance and then swings away up the hillside.

Leave the track at this point and take a narrow path which goes through a clump of bushes beside the water. This will bring you to a stile. Cross it and turn sharp right on to a path which follows the field fence on the right.

At the end of the field turn left to follow a faint grassy track that goes down towards the old church. The church, which today is little more than a chapel, is all that remains of the village church featured in Falkner's novel. In it are to be seen two fine memorial brasses belonging to the Mohun family and a small plaque to the memory of John Meade Falkner.

The track turns right beside the churchyard wall and then forks. Keep to the left-hand branch which continues along the wall to a gate. Go through the gate and walk past the cottages on the left up to the road.

Turn left and walk along the road back to the car. This will take you past the new church which was completed in 1829.

Walk 28   The Hardy Monument

3½ miles (5·5 km)

OS sheet 194
Start: the Hardy Monument

The Hardy Monument is a rather unimpressive grey stone tower which stands high on the slopes of Black Down. It was erected in 1844 to the memory of Admiral Sir Thomas Masterman Hardy who was captain of Nelson's flagship, the *Victory*, during the Battle of Trafalgar.

The village of Portesham is a place which the Admiral knew well for it was near here that he spent his boyhood. Although perhaps not the most beautiful of the Dorset villages it has a charm of its own. There is a delightful duck pond set beside a small village green and a fifteenth-century church.

One of the most outstanding features of this walk is the scenery. Although the flight of steps which once gave access to the platform at the top of the Hardy Monument is now closed, there are still magnificent views to be seen from the heathland at its base and from several other vantage points throughout the walk. On a clear day the walker can enjoy a constantly changing panorama which includes Weymouth, Portland, the Chesil Beach and St Catherine's Chapel at Abbotsbury.

Take the A35 trunk road towards Bridport from Dorchester and turn left in Winterbourne Abbas on to the Martinstown road, then turn right to follow the signs to the Hardy Monument. Around the base of the monument there is a wide expanse of open ground which provides plenty of free parking.

Near the point where the track which gives access to the open ground around the monument joins the road, a secondary track leads down the hill to the right. Take this track: within less than a hundred yards it forks. Keep to the right-hand fork which almost immediately joins another track in a T-junction. Turn right and follow this track which curves gently to the right and eventually rejoins the road. Turn left at this point on to another track leading steeply down the hill. After a short distance it passes through a gateway where the gate is broken and continues to go down the hill through a wood.

Near the bottom of the hill a narrow path joins the track from the left and not long afterwards the track divides into three. Keep to the centre track which continues down the hill through the trees.

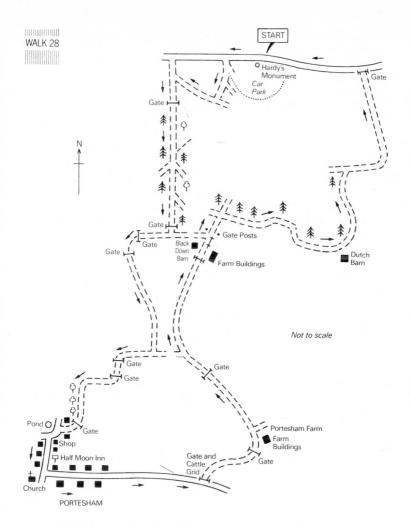

As it emerges from the mature part of the wood the track forks again. This time take the right-hand branch, which is grass covered and leads through a nursery of young fir trees to a gateway.

Beyond the gateway the track joins another rather indistinct track at right-angles. Turn right and follow this track to a metal field gate set in a wall. Go through the gate and turn left to cross the corner of the field and pass through a second metal gate on to a grassy track which leads up the hill beside the fence on the left.

At the top of the slope follow the track to the right. After running along beside a wall on the left for some distance it passes through a

91

gateway and continues to follow the wall down a slope towards a second gate.

Beyond this gate the track swings right to curve round the perimeter of the field and descend the hill by some trees on the far side. This leads you to a gate at the bottom right-hand corner of the field which gives access to a gravel track that runs down between some houses to the road.

Turn left and follow the road through Portesham village bearing left at the shop into Front Street and passing the Half Moon Inn on the left. Just beyond the inn turn left into Winters Lane. It is sign-posted Coryates, The Waddons and Upwey.

Winters Lane leads up the hill out of the village. Just where it flattens out a track leads over a cattle grid to the left. It is marked 'Bridleway. Hardy's Monument $1\frac{1}{2}$'. Go through the metal gate beside the cattle grid and follow the track up the slope. At the top it bends to the left, passes through another metal gate and skirts Portesham Farm buildings on the right.

Near the far corner of the farm buildings it is joined by another track from the right. Ignore this and carry straight on. After passing through another metal gate the track leads down the hill to Black Down Barn. Here it runs through yet another gateway and forks.

Take the right-hand fork; it leads up the hill and at the top of the primary slope is crossed by a second track. Turn right and follow this track which leads straight along the side of the hill between a nursery of small fir trees to the left and open fields to the right.

After some distance the track swings round in a sharp loop and then passes a Dutch barn on the right. Beyond this it turns to the left to head towards the Hardy Monument which stands on the sky-line.

The track goes straight ahead for some way and then merges with another from the left. Turn right and follow this down a gentle slope, pausing on the way to admire the beautiful views of Weymouth and Portland to the right.

At the bottom of the slope the track swings left and follows the valley. This will take you back to the road. On reaching it turn left and walk up the hill to the monument and the parking area.

Walk 29   Golden Cap

$3\frac{1}{2}$ miles (5·5 km)

OS sheet 193
Start: Langdon Hill

Golden Cap is the highest cliff on the south coast. It is 617 ft high and
forms part of a piece of coastline known as the Golden Cap Estate
which is owned by the National Trust. This is a particularly lovely
area and the summit of Golden Cap makes a very good vantage point
from which to enjoy its beauty.

The cliffs are especially worthy of mention for no two are alike.
Greensand, limestone and clay combine to give them an endless
variety of colours and shades. Yet, even amongst such a wealth of
colouring, Golden Cap stands out because of its unique beauty. The
top section of it is composed of greensand and is bright gold in colour.

Take the A35 trunk road from Bridport travelling towards Lyme
Regis. Turn left just before you come to the dual carriageway at the
top of the hill beyond Chideock and then almost immediately left
again on to the track to Langdon Hill. Where the track branches take
the right-hand fork. This will lead you up to the car park.

Leave the car park by the gate on the right-hand side near the car
park sign and follow the track. It curves round the hillside and then
emerges from the trees for a short distance, giving good views of the
coast towards Lyme Regis.

As the trees close in once more a second track joins it from the left
but ignore this and carry straight on. Follow the track until it curves
left again and you pass a seat on the right. Just beyond this turn right
on to a narrow path signposted to Golden Cap.

Go round the barrier at the bottom of the slope and turn right
through a gate into a field. Head obliquely right to a gate in the hedge
at the far side then follow the path straight ahead keeping the fence on
your left.

At the corner of the fence keep to the path which curves right and
descends the hill to a gate in the left-hand corner of the field. Go
through this and follow the footpath straight ahead. After a while it
broadens into a track and is joined by another from the left, but ignore
this and go on past a ruined building on your right to a gate. Beyond
this the track leads down to St Gabriel's House where it meets three
other tracks.

Take the track straight ahead which goes down a slight slope and
through a gate. It is joined by a footpath to the right and then swings

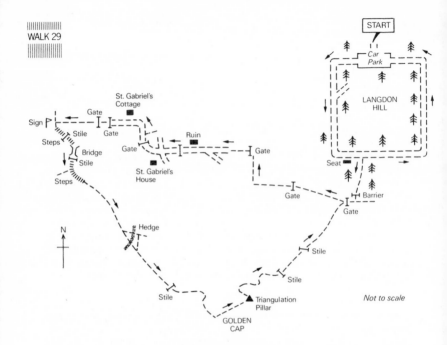

left to pass the front of St Gabriel's Cottage. From this point continue to follow the track straight ahead ignoring two gates on the right. This will bring you to a gate at the far side of the field which is connected by a short fenced path to a second gate. Go through these and then follow the hedge on the left to the signpost marked 'Coastal Path'.

Turn left on to the path which descends some steps into a gully. Cross the bridge over the stream and, where the path divides, half-way up the steps on the far side, keep to the left. At the end of the steps take the path straight ahead to the top of the primary slope. Then follow the edge of the cliff on your right up towards Golden Cap.

Where the path passes through the hedge take the left-hand fork for easier access and then turn sharp right to continue the climb to a stile at the top of the field. From here a path leads up through the undergrowth to the summit of Golden Cap.

At the top it is worth a small diversion to the right to enjoy the magnificent views before turning left to follow the path to a triangulation pillar. Turn left again at the pillar and follow the path down the hill to a stile. Go over this and cross the field to a second stile. Cross it and follow the hedge on the right down to the gate in the corner of the field.

Beyond the gate turn left round the barrier to follow the path back up the slope. Where it joins the track turn right. The track winds round the hillside and will bring you back to the car park.

Walk 30   Stonebarrow Hill

3½ miles (5.5 km)

OS sheet 193
Start: Stonebarrow Hill

The area in which this walk is situated is part of the Golden Cap Estate which is owned by the National Trust. It is a place of great natural beauty composed of softly rolling hills and rugged cliffs from which there are magnificent views.

Parts of the estate consist of open heathland, but the majority of it is farmed. The farmers use the more traditional methods and this means that a great amount of wild-life is able to survive here. There is a wide selection of wild flowers, a large variety of birds including buzzards and kestrels, mammals such as badgers and foxes and, in summer, an abundance of brightly coloured butterflies and other insects.

Turn off the A35 trunk road at the bottom of the hill just east of Charmouth on to a narrow lane called Stonebarrow Lane. The lane goes up a hill, crosses a cattle grid and degenerates into an unmetalled track. There is a National Trust sign on the right and just beyond it is a wide expanse of grass which provides ample space for parking.

Carry on along the track, passing the National Trust information centre on the left. When you reach the place where the track, having been joined by another from the right, goes over a cattle grid, turn right to go through the small gate by the National Trust sign.

Just beyond this gate the path forks. Take the left-hand fork which runs along the hill-top skirting some bushes on the left. This will bring you to another small gate and not far beyond it the path cuts through a low bank and divides. Follow the right-hand branch which curves round to the brow of the hill. From here carry on down the slope and through a gateway to a track in the valley below.

Turn left, go through another gate and follow the track past the farmhouse on the right and a cottage on the left. This will bring you to a farmyard. Turn left to follow the cottage wall and then go through the left of the two farm gates on to the track beyond.

When you come to where the track is joined by three others turn right on to the one marked with a National Trust sign labelled 'St Gabriel's'. Follow this track which winds down into the valley passing a gate on the left marked 'Campers' Cars Only', then carry on up a short slope to St Gabriel's House. Here four tracks meet. Turn on to the one which leads sharply away to the right, go through the gate and, ignoring the narrow footpath that ascends a flight of steps to the

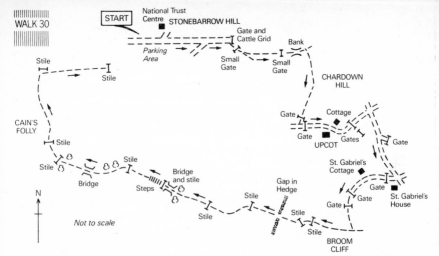

right, walk on past St Gabriel's Cottage. Beyond this carry straight on passing two field gates on the right, to reach a gate at the far side of the field. Go through this gate which is closely followed by another at the end of a short stretch of fenced path and then follow the hedge on the left to a signpost marked 'Coastal Path'.

Turn right and walk up the slope to go over a stile in the hedge. Turn slightly left and cross the corner of the field to a second stile. From here the path leads slightly to the right, heading for a gap in the hedge near the far left-hand corner of the field. Go through it and carry straight on to another stile at the top of the slope. Cross this and bear left to follow the curve of the cliff to the next stile ignoring a gate across the field to the right.

After this stile head straight down the hill to the bottom. Ignore a stile to the right and follow the path on through the scrub towards the gully. This will bring you to a bridge with a stile on the far side of it and beyond this a flight of steps which lead up out of the gully.

At the top of the steps bear slightly right to follow the path to yet another stile and then go straight ahead down the hill keeping the edge of the cliff on your left. Cross the small stream in the valley and carry on up the next slope keeping to the left of two clumps of brambles. Continue along the cliff crossing a narrow footbridge and climbing another slope to where a narrow path leads straight ahead through some bushes. This will lead you to another stile beyond which is a field. Carry on up the slope to another stile at the far side of the field and then follow the path up the hill through the bushes. It is a steep climb but well worth it as the views from the top are magnificent.

After a short pause cross the ridge and head towards another stile but turn right just before it, by the National Trust sign marked 'Cain's Folly'. Follow the footpath which runs along beside the fence until you come to a stile set in the hedge straight ahead. Cross this and you are back on the expanse of grass which serves as a parking area.